GIVING GOD YOUR FUTURE

women of faith™

GIVING GOD YOUR FUTURE

BY

CHRISTA KINDE

FOREWORD BY

THELMA WELLS

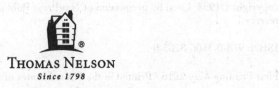

THOMAS NELSON
Since 1798

Previously Published as *Giving God Your All*.

The publishers are grateful to Christa Kinde for her collaboration, writing skills, and editorial help in developing the content for this book.

Published in Nashville, Tennessee by Thomas Nelson.
Thomas Nelson is a registered trademark of harper Collins Christian Publishing, Inc.

Thomas Nelson titles may be purchased in bulk for educational, business, fund-raising, or sales promotional use. For information, please e-mail SpecialMarkets@ ThomasNelson.com.

Scripture quotations marked NKJV are taken from The Holy Bible, The New King James Version (NKJV®), copyright 1979, 1980, 1982, Thomas Nelson Publishers. Used by permission. All rights reserved.

Scripture quotations marked NLT are taken from The Holy Bible, The New Living Translation (NLT). Copyright © 1986 by the Tyndale House Publishers, Wheaton, Illinois, 60189. Used by permission. All rights reserved.

Scripture quotations marked ncv are taken from The Holy Bible, New Century Version®. Copyright © 1987, 1988, 1991 by Word Publishing, a Division of Thomas Nelson. Used by permission. All rights reserved.

Scripture quotations marked KJV are taken from The Holy Bible, The King James Version of the Bible.

Scripture quotations marked MSG are taken from The Holy Bible, The Message (MSG), copyright ©1993. Used by permission of NavPress Publishing Group. All rights reserved.

ISBN: 978-0-3106-8263-9

First Printing May 2016 / Printed in the United States of America

⚐ CONTENTS ☙

Contents

⫸ FOREWORD ⫷

Have you ever said what I've said: "Girl, I can't give everything to God. I don't know what He would want me to do. He might want to send me to Africa, and I don't like flies." Okay, I'm not proud I said that. But when I said it, I really meant it. Fear had me bound—the fear of God telling me to do something that I either did not want to do or something that was not convenient. Shame on me.

I'm glad God is a merciful God. He just let me go on with that nonsense until my spirit could take it no more. One night in 1955, the Holy Spirit of God convicted me to the point of falling on my face and surrendering all of me and mine to God. When I got up from the floor, I knew without a shadow of a doubt that God had accepted my repentance and my submission. And yes, He did send me to Africa, but I was not bothered one bit by flies. From that night to this day, I have attempted to lay it all on the altar before God and to submit to His will for my life.

This courageous study will help you to become willing to trust God with your everything because He is the God of everything. Whatever you're going through, God knew about it before He divided the water from the land, flung stars in space, and grew mighty trees. It's true. He is the Alpha (the beginning) and the Omega (the ending) of your experiences in life.

After I gave God my all, I was sitting around talking to some other women—presidents of companies, entrepreneurs, computer gurus, and power brokers. They asked each one in the meeting to share their goals for the coming year. I listened to them talk and share their financial goals, career goals, personal goals, and so forth. When they got to me without any shame, I said, "I have no goals for next year. In the past, every time I made goals for the coming year, I noticed that by February God had changed them. That was frustrating and fulfilling for me. Frustrating because I had spent valuable time, energy, and resources to develop my goals that went out of the window when God changed them. Fulfilling because when I turned my life over to God and gave Him my all, I realized that whatever He had for me to do was His will for my life. I no longer had to figure out what to do—I just had to do it when I was told to by God. So my goals for the year became deadlines for what I had to do.

It sure makes life a lot easier to handle when all the responsibility of planning your future is left up to the Master of the Future. Deadlines without self-imposed duties are less stressful and more manageable. It requires knowing who our Leader is, understanding the causes and effects of our unwillingness to give God our all, throwing away our alibis, accepting the promises of God, trusting the only One who knows all our stuff, and saying "bye-bye" to our desire to control our lives.

It's hard but it can be done. Just ask Miss I-Can't-Surrender-Everything-to-God—me. Once I did it and saw the benefits from it, I was hooked on the only Stronghold in my life now, Almighty God. I'm glad His ways are not my ways and His thoughts are not my thoughts. Thank goodness for that, ' cause this world would be a plum mess if it were left up to me. At the end of this study, you will be able to say with conviction, "All to Jesus I Surrender."

—*Thelma Wells*

⚹ INTRODUCTION ⚹

Are you familiar with the story *The Emperor's New Clothes*? Two cunning con artists are able to fleece an entire nation because nobody wants to look foolish. They set themselves up as master tailors and offer to create a new suit of clothes for the emperor. The emperor, being a trifle vain, is enormously pleased at the prospect of new finery...until the first fitting. With a knowing gleam in their eyes, the conniving tailors display their handiwork, made from a most remarkable fabric. This cloth is so fine, so rare, so miraculously wrought that only the best of men can see it. Those who are unable to see it are fools, unworthy of the position they hold. The emperor is stunned! He'd never considered himself a fool, but for the life of him he cannot see a thing in the tailor's hands. And so he pretends he can see what the others claim to hold. And so do all his friends and associates, for no one wants to seem a fool!

The suit of clothes is then "completed," and the emperor agrees to parade through the land, showing off his new attire. But in the end, the truth comes out. There is no cloth. There are no clothes. Everyone has been pretending to see what was not there to begin with, rather than stand out as the only one who could not see.

Have you ever had a secret suspicion that you're missing out on something important in your Christian walk? This believer or that believer will talk about their walk of faith with words like *vibrant, intimate,* and *personal.* Their glowing description of their relationship with the divine makes you wonder if you're doing something wrong. Oh, you have faith. You do love God. But to call your dealings with the Lord *vibrant* would be going a little too far. You're not sure what to expect, but you know it's not this. But who wants to look foolish? If everyone else says their Christian life is so intimate and personal, ours had better be, too. So we all use the same words. We all nod with understanding when a friend shares about God's working in their hearts. But we wonder why God seems more an acquaintance than a friend to us.

What changes a life of nodding acquaintance to one of personal intimacy? In a word—dependence. Once we're willing to trust God in every situation, seek His opinions over any others, trust Him in every circumstance, and do what he would do—then the relationship we long for deepens, strengthens, and becomes vibrant.

This study takes a look at what the Bible says about trusting God enough to give Him our all, and being able to say, "Not my will, but Yours be done." We'll see that only He can empower us to live a life like that, and as we give Him our all, He gives us everything we need to have an intimate, growing, personal relationship with Him.

CHAPTER ONE

TAKE ME TO YOUR LEADER

"THE LORD IS MY SHEPHERD, I SHALL NOT WANT."

Psalm 23:1 NKJV

You're standing in line, arms loaded down with packages, inching your way towards the customer service counter. Your list of tasks and questions is long—a couple of returns, an exchange, a rain check, and an inquiry about the store's gift registry for your daughter. It's your last errand of the morning, and it'll be a relief to get it all done. Finally it's your turn, and as you step forward, you groan inwardly. The clerk's face wears an uncertain smile, and her smock sports a badge with block letters—"Trainee."

The next several minutes become a test to every one of your Christian virtues. First, she botches the returns. Then, you find out she's never done an exchange before. Next, she can't find the gift registry forms, and she's never even heard of a rain check. Will your morning end with an exercise in futility? But then you hear those blissful words, "Let me call my manager."

CLEARING ⤢ THE ⤡ COBWEBS

Have you ever had a mentor—a person who showed you the ropes when you were starting something new?

1

There are times when we don't want to waste time dickering with someone who isn't in charge. We want to deal with the one who is in charge. We need someone who knows what's going on, knows what they're talking about, and knows what to do next. We want someone with the authority to take charge, make decisions, and effect changes. So we say, "Take me to your leader."

1. Let's take a quick look at the Lord's qualifications as "upper level management."

- What rather majestic titles does Paul give to God in 1 Timothy 6:15?

- How is Jesus described in Revelation 17:14?

- In Revelation 19:16, Jesus wears His name clearly. Is it "Trainee"? What is it?

2. God's authority is unquestioned, and His ability to lead unparalleled. Match up these psalms, which pray for and thank God for His leading in our lives.

____ Psalm 5:8   a. For Your name's sake, lead me and guide me.

____ Psalm 25:5   b. Lead me in the land of uprightness.

____ Psalm 31:3   c. Lead me, O LORD, in Your righteousness.

____ Psalm 43:3   d. Lead me in the way everlasting.

____ Psalm 139:10   e. Let Your light and Your truth lead me.

____ Psalm 139:24   f. Lead me in Your truth and teach me.

____ Psalm 143:10   g. Your right hand shall lead me and hold me.

3. Consider the theme that runs through the next three verses. What do each of them compare with the leading of the Lord?

Numbers 27:17 — "Who may go out before them and go in before them, who may _____ them out and _____ them in, that the congregation of the LORD may not be like _____ which have no _____" (NKJV).

Psalm 80:1 — "Give ear, O _____ of Israel, You who _____ Joseph like a _____" (NKJV).

Isaiah 40:11 — "He will _____ His _____ like a _____; He will _____ the _____ with His arm, And _____ them in His bosom, and _____ _____ those who are with young" (NKJV).

4. One of the most familiar chapters in all of Scripture begins, "The Lord is my shepherd" (Ps. 23:1 NKJV). God leads us, just as a shepherd leads his flock of sheep. What happens to sheep who have no shepherd—no leader—according to Zechariah 10:2?

5. According to Matthew 9:36, what characteristic of the multitudes that followed Jesus touched His heart with compassion?

There's nothing more endearing than a little lamb in the springtime, frisking and dancing in the meadows for the sheer joy of living. But Scripture's comparison of us to sheep is not entirely flattering. Sheep are useful creatures, true enough. But sheep are also skittish, gullible, defenseless, short-sighted, and rather smelly. Can you imagine walking up to a milling flock of sheep and asking, "Who's in charge here?" And from the midst of the flock comes a bleating voice, "That would be me!" But how could that sheep lead, when she cannot even see past the wooly rumps that surround her? She cannot guide the flock, protect the flock, or shelter the flock because she's just one of the flock. Sheep need a shepherd— one who can see over the flocks and oversee their care.

> "Jesus prayed, 'Not My will, but Thine be done.' That's the most terrifying prayer in all of Scripture."
>
> Nicole Johnson

6. Sheep may not be the brightest animals in God's creation, but there's one thing they do know! What do these verses say it is?

• John 10:4–5

• John 10:27

7. From the very beginning, the prophets foretold that Messiah would lead His people—"But you, Bethlehem . . . out of you shall come a Ruler Who will shepherd My people Israel" (Matt. 2:6 NKJV).

• What does Jesus call Himself in John 10:11–14?

• How does Peter describe Jesus in 1 Peter 2:25?

• What title does 1 Peter 5:4 give to the Lord at His coming?

8. We can't be both sheep and shepherd. When we've determined to give God our all, we must accept His leadership in our lives. Where do these verses tell us the Lord will lead?

• Isaiah 42:16

- Isaiah 49:10

> *"I've always found it hard to delegate. This spills over into my relationship with Christ. Doing makes me feel as if progress is being made—though that isn't necessarily so."*
>
> **Sheila Walsh**

- Revelation 7:17

9. We have a Shepherd who knows the way, but the fact of His presence isn't enough. The Shepherd can only lead those who are willing to follow! What does Jesus urge us to do in John 12:26?

DIGGING DEEPER

There are many more verses in the Scriptures that talk about shepherds and shepherding. Here are just a few more, if you'd like to dig a little deeper.

- Psalm 28:9

- Ezekiel 34:12, 23–24

- John 10:16

- Hebrews 13:20

PONDER & PRAY

Some of us prefer to lead, and some of us would rather follow. But for anyone, it can be hard to submit to the leadership of others—especially if we do not trust them or we do not like the direction they are headed. This week, ponder over the lessons we can learn from the humble sheep and their relationship with the shepherd. Pray for an ear to hear the voice of your Shepherd. Pray for a heart that will not wander, but is willing to follow so that you will not go astray. Remember how much you are dearly loved by the Shepherd of your soul.

TRINKETS TO TREASURE

At the close of each lesson, you will be presented with a small gift. Though imaginary, it will serve to remind you of the things you have learned. Think of it as a souvenir. Souvenirs are little trinkets we pick up on our journeys to remind us of where we have been. They keep us from forgetting the path we have traveled. Hide these little treasures in your heart, for as you ponder them, they will draw you closer to God.

Before we can confidently give God our all, we must be sure that He will take good care of the life we are putting in His hands. Just as a sheep must know and trust its shepherd, we must know and trust God completely. He is our Good Shepherd, and so our trinket this week is a shepherd's crook, to remind us that the Lord will lead us aright.

CHAPTER TWO

PLANS AND AGENDAS

"IF THIS PLAN OR THIS WORK IS OF MEN, IT WILL
COME TO NOTHING; BUT IF IT IS OF GOD, YOU
CANNOT OVERTHROW IT."

Acts 5:38–39 NKJV

*I*f you have been married for any length of time, you have undoubtedly encountered times when your priorities don't line up with the priorities of your husband. Maybe it's a Saturday afternoon, for example, and you see a number of things that need to be tended to around the house. The leaves in the backyard need raked. A hinge on the front door needs to be fixed. There are some boxes sitting in the living room that need to be taken to the attic. As you look around, you see many other things that need attention.

These tasks, you decide, are your priorities for the day. But to get them all done, you will need some help from your husband. It is time to divide and conquer! But unfortunately, you quickly discover your husband has his own priorities for the day. It seems that today is the big game between his alma mater and their biggest rival, and there is *no way* he can miss it. He is camped out in the den, the television on, his feet propped up, and a chilled beverage close at hand.

CLEARING ↗ THE ↖ COBWEBS

Primetime sitcoms have introduced us to many a TV family. Do you have a favorite husband-wife duo, past or present?

When you go through your list with him, he promises that he will start to work on it at halftime and finish up everything once the game is over. Even if he is always true to his word, it's still aggravating to see him sit there *doing nothing* while there is so much to be done around the house! If only his priorities matched your own, you could get so much work done that day.

We women usually have some kind of plans like these in mind, and we don't like having our plans postponed for any reason. And that's where we often run into trouble with the Lord. Quite often, His plans for our lives aren't exactly what we had in mind. But when we're learning to give God our all, we must realize that all our lives—even our schedule and life goals—are in His hands.

1. When we have a plan, and God has a plan, and those two plans don't seem to be matching up, we are mightily tempted to ignore God's plan altogether. What do Psalm 9:17 (NLT) and Galatians 6:7 (NLT) warn about living as if God weren't there?

> "Jesus continues to be a redeemer, and He can use my disappointing situation for purposes beyond my understanding."
>
> Patsy Clairmont

2. Have you ever made a willful choice against God? How do the people in Jeremiah 18:12 decide to live their lives?

3. God is aware of our wandering hearts. He lets us make our own choices. But we are warned that the plans we make apart from God are doomed from the start.

- Why do people's plans fail, according to Isaiah 22:11 (NLT)?

- What happens to those who try to hide their plans from God, according to Isaiah 29:15 (NLT)?

- What is certain for those who are contrary and rebellious to God?

4. When Jesus had risen from the dead and all of Jerusalem was in an uproar over it, the Jewish leaders gathered together to try to decide what to do. In Acts 5:38–39, what were the wise words that dictated the Sanhedrin's decision?

5. You can't get around the sovereignty of God. He sees all, knows all, and can do all He plans. What do each of these verses tell us about God's plans and the plans of mere mortals?

- Psalm 33:10

- Proverbs 16:9

- Proverbs 19:21

*I*f you want to get anything done in life, you have to make plans. We're told to make lists, set realistic goals, and keep track of our progress. We need a one-year plan, a five-year plan, and a ten-year plan. We're supposed to have a financial plan—college funds, retirement funds, investment funds. We're supposed to be on a Bible reading plan, a Scripture memorization schedule, and the women's missions planning committee. Our calendars are locked up from week to week with school schedules, sports schedules, church events, and appointments. Sometimes, it feels as if our lives plan themselves!

But in the middle of all this hubbub of daily life, our heart has its own plans, dreams, expectations, and attitudes. These are what guide our decisions and choices. And this is the part of us—the heart of us—that we can give to God.

6. David was delighted that God had so many plans for his life. What does he express gratitude for in Psalm 40:5 (NLT)?

7. What does the psalmist say about God's plans for us in Psalm 138:8 (NLT)?

> "Jesus said, 'Follow me.' His desire is that His Word and His Spirit be our guides for this life. Being a follower of Jesus Christ means becoming more and more like Him—letting His Spirit transform us into all we were created to be. That happens, dear friend, from the inside out."
>
> Luci Swindoll

8. There is comfort in the fact that the Lord is changeless. He's dependably the same no matter what our circumstances might be. The same can be said of His plans. What does Psalm 33:11 tell us about God's plans?

> "How do we truly give up our agendas? How do we genuinely say, 'Not my will but Yours, Lord'? For me, the answer to that question is found in my understanding and acceptance of God's sovereignty."
>
> Marilyn Meberg

9. When we give our plans and agendas over into God's capable hands, we needn't fear. What does Jeremiah 29:11 (NLT) tell us God has planned for us?

DIGGING DEEPER

There's a song many of us have known since we were children. Simple, yet profound, it tells us, "He's got the whole world in His hands." This theme is found throughout Scripture. Job said, "Isn't it clear that they all know and agree that God is sovereign, that he holds all things in his hands" (Job 12:9 MSG). If, indeed, all things are in the Lord's hands, what kinds of things in your life can you trust in His hands?

PONDER & PRAY

During the week ahead, ponder over the state of your heart. Ask yourself honestly, "Have I been so wrapped up in my own plans and agendas that I've given no thought to God's?" We have been assured by Scripture that God's plans are good and that nothing can stand in their way. Ask the Lord for a heart willing to shape its agenda around His plans.

TRINKETS TO TREASURE

Our trinket this week is a feather duster to remind us that we must always submit our plans and priorities to God. There will be times when the Lord's plans will run contrary to our own, and there may even be times when it seems as if God isn't doing anything that we think needs to be done. During these moments, rather than be impatient, we need to trust God. He will do what is good and right when the proper time comes.

NOTES & PRAYER REQUESTS

_____

_____

_____

_____

_____

_____

_____

_____

_____

_____

_____

_____

_____

_____

_____

_____

_____

_____

_____

CHAPTER THREE

IT'S MY LIFE

"NEVERTHELESS NOT MY WILL, BUT YOURS, BE DONE."

Luke 22:42 NKJV

*I*n today's society, we are taught that our lives are our own. *See for yourself. Decide for yourself. Be yourself. Express yourself. Pamper yourself. Have faith in yourself. Be in touch with yourself. Be sure of yourself. Believe in yourself. Be true to yourself. When making choices, we're urged to look within for our answers. Listen to your heart. Trust your instincts. Follow your heart. You've earned it. You deserve it. You owe it to yourself.*

Self-interest is molded into positive character qualities—self-assured, self-possessed, self-reliant. Selfish choices are applauded. We are born with the desire to put our own interests ahead of anyone else's, and then we learn that this attitude is socially acceptable. Is it any wonder so many of us struggle with hearts that are self-serving, self-righteous, and self-satisfied?

CLEARING ☞ THE ☜ COBWEBS

Have you ever had anyone in your life that loved to spoil you?

1. When it comes to surrendering our lives into God's hands, we're often faced with a battle of the wills. My will vs. God's will. And it can be the fight of the century! What does 1 Peter 4:2 say we should live for?

"Surrendering our agenda for our lives is the hardest thing we will do."

Nicole Johnson

2. God called David "a man after My own heart." According to Acts 13:22, what was David willing to do?

3. Submitting our will to God's isn't always easy to do. In Luke 22:42, what were Jesus' famous words when He gave His all to His Father?

4. There are promises and blessings connected to those who do with will of God.

• What does Jesus call those who do God's will in Mark 3:35?

• What does 1 John 2:17 say about those who do the will of God?

5. There's a distinct line between willful and willing. When we give our all to God, we must be willing to put what He wants above what we want. How does Ephesians 6:6 describe such an attitude?

> "Surrendering to God is the key that unlocks the door to the life you want. A bigger spiritual 'to do' list or a calendar full of church activities will not change our lives. When we give ourselves to God—mind, body, soul, and spirit—He changes us."
>
> Nicole Johnson

*W*hen we were babies, our parents couldn't wait for us to say our first words. Invariably, we thrilled our parents by gurgling out an indistinct, "Mama" or "Dada." But not long after that, we learned the next two words in a toddler's vocabulary—"No" and "Mine." We exert our independence by the time we can stand on our own two feet.

Independence—it's a part of growing up. Individuality—it's what makes us *us*! But we're foolish if we begin demanding our rights as individuals without once considering the One who made us uniquely us! He made us the way we are to suit His own purposes. Learning to give God our all means learning that our lives are not entirely our own.

6. In fact, if we're believers, our lives are not our own.

- What does Deuteronomy 32:6 say that God did for His people?

- According to 1 Corinthians 7:23, what one word describes the state of the believer?

- What does Paul say is the consequence of this position, according to 1 Corinthians 6:20?

7. What was the price of our salvation, according to Galatians 3:13?

> *"Our impatience to have God move now, to act in ways that make sense to us, will drive us to take control of our lives. God is moving in ways that we cannot see or understand. This means we are left with the question, 'Do I trust Him?'"*
>
> **Sheila Walsh**

8. *Redeemed* is an interesting word, which in Scripture could be paraphrased as *purchased* or *exchanged*. We have been bought. We are redeemed.

Isaiah 44:22 — "I have _____ _____, like a thick _____, your _____, And like a _____, your _____. Return to Me, for I have _____ you" (NKJV).

Isaiah 43:1 — "But now, thus says the LORD, who _____ you, O Jacob, And He who _____ you, O Israel: 'Fear not, for I have _____ you; I have _____ you by your _____; You are _____" (NKJV).

Psalm 71:23 — "My _____ shall _____ _____ when I _____ to You, And my _____, which You have _____" (NKJV).

9. We belong to God! It's a beautiful truth if we have a willing heart. What was the advice that an aged David passed along to his son, Solomon, when the time came to pass down the crown? It's found in 1 Chronicles 28:9—and he speaks of willingness.

DIGGING DEEPER

In this chapter we have discussed our willfulness, our willingness, and the will of God. Here are a few more verses which touch on each of these subjects. Look them up for a little more study.

- Psalm 40:8

- Psalm 143:10

- Matthew 23:37

- John 6:38

- Romans 12:2

- Colossians 4:12

PONDER & PRAY

This week, as you ponder over the many verses we've studied, pray that any small areas of willfulness in your heart be exchanged for willingness. Our lives are not our own, but we must still present them to the Lord. Tell the Lord how much you want to live for Him. Ask Him to show you how you can make your life a living sacrifice for His glory. He knows how much you need Him to make this a reality.

TRINKETS TO TREASURE

You have been bought, and so your trinket for the week is a gold coin. Of course the price of your life was much higher than that of mere gold. Jesus' lifeblood was spilled to pay the price. So now you belong to God, though you don't always act like it. Your bit of gold will serve to remind you that you can no longer live, willfully serving yourself. Now, you live for the One who saved you, willingly for His glory.

NOTES & PRAYER REQUESTS

CHAPTER FOUR

WHAT DO I HAVE TO OFFER?

"OFFER THE SACRIFICES OF RIGHTEOUSNESS, AND PUT YOUR TRUST IN THE LORD."

Psalm 4:5 NKJV

hen I was growing up, the last day of school before Christmas break was always the day when our class had its Christmas party. There would be cookies and cupcakes and red Kool-Aid. We'd have to bring in a small present marked "boy" or "girl" for the gift exchange. And then, there'd be a procession up to the desk as we carried our presents for the teacher to place on her desk. These gifts were opened with some ceremony, and each was exclaimed over—mugs, ornaments, potpourri, chocolates, stationary.

I suppose every teacher receives such things in quantity over the course of their careers. But my gift wasn't a pretty mug with an apple on it that said "#1 Teacher," because my mother always sent me to school with a homemade gift. Each of my teachers always received a loaf of my mother's special Christmastime cherry pecan bread. I loved that bread. It was one of my holiday favorites. And

CLEARING THE COBWEBS

What is one of the most memorable Christmas gifts you've ever received?

my mother was a good cook, so I knew my teacher would like the present. But sitting up there on the desk, my small loaf wrapped in aluminum foil with a little ribbon stuck on top looked kind of humble. Store-bought gifts came in pretty boxes with bright wrap and tissue paper. My teacher never even opened my present. She just had to read the label and move on. What I had to offer was the best I could give, but in comparison with everything else, it seemed paltry, insignificant, small.

Sometimes we hesitate to give God our all by telling ourselves we've got nothing to give. Or that what we have is too humble to be worth much. After all, God has so many other vibrant, talented, good people to choose from! Can just one person—*me*—really matter, make a difference?

> "When our souls ask deep questions, such as, Are you making a difference? We try to answer those questions with our 'to do' list. 'See,' we say as we show our list, 'we're getting a lot done.'"
>
> Nicole Johnson

1. We may not understand how God can use what we have to offer, but give it we must! What did Jesus tell His followers to give to God in Matthew 22:21 (NLT)?

2. So then, what belongs to God?

- What does 2 Corinthians 1:20 (NLT) say that we must give to God?

- What does Ephesians 5:20 (NLT) tell us we need to give to God?

3. These things are good and true, but God doesn't stop there. What does Deuteronomy 10:12–13 say that we must give to the Lord?

> *"If we will relinquish control of our lives and place our trust in God with absolute confidence then the peace of God, which is beyond human understanding, will cover us, protecting our hearts and minds."*
>
> Sheila Walsh

4. In Psalm 78:8 (NLT) we find a negative example. David tells us here how *not* to live. What do these people withhold from God, and how is their character described?

5. God has an understandable desire for us to give Him our all. The Scriptures urge us to do things wholeheartedly!

Deuteronomy 4:29 — "You will _____ the Lord your God, and you will _____ Him if you _____ Him with all your heart and with all your soul" (NKJV).

Deuteronomy 6:5 — "You shall _____ the Lord your God with all your heart" (NKJV).

Deuteronomy 10:12 — "To _____ the Lord your God with all your heart and with all your soul" (NKJV).

Deuteronomy 30:2 — "_____ to the Lord your God and _____ His voice . . . with all your heart and soul" (NKJV).

Deuteronomy 30:10 — "_____ to the Lord your God with all your heart and with all your soul" (NKJV).

Psalm 86:12 — "With all my heart I will _____ _____" (NLT).

Jeremiah 29:13 — "_____ for Me with all your heart" (NKJV).

*T*here's a simple poem that's been put to song. It's called, "What Can I Give Him?" Many of us probably learned it as a part of some Christmas program back in our elementary days. Look at its matter-of-fact approach:

> *What can I give Him,*
> *poor as I am*
> *If I were a Shepherd*
> *I would give a lamb,*
> *If I were a wise man*
> *I would do my part,*
> *But what can I give Him,*
> *I'll give Him my heart.*

We may not feel we have much to bring to the Lord, but that doesn't matter. He doesn't require of us things we do not have. He only wants what rightfully belongs to Him. All He wants of us is a whole-hearted willingness to do His will. He wants us to give Him our hearts.

6. Are we unfailing in giving to God what we owe Him? Does our heart belong to Him? Does He receive all our thanks? Do we give Him all the glory? What about our lives—do we live for Him? What do these verses say we must do one day?

- Ecclesiastes 11:9 (NLT)

- Matthew 12:36

- Romans 14:12 (NLT)

7. With this in mind, what does Paul plead with believers to do in Romans 6:13 (NLT)?

8. How is this idea rephrased in Romans 12:1 (NLT)?

> *"An authentic life and self is one in which the layers on the outside are merely expressions of the core on the inside. The core on the inside is what we surrender to God."*
>
> Nicole Johnson

9. What a good question! "Is this too much to ask?" (Rom. 12:1 NLT). What does God ask of us? Everything! We give ourselves into His hands with our whole heart. But our relationship with the Lord is not one-sided. By His Spirit, he enables us to give something back. What do these verses say about the work of God in our hearts?

- Jeremiah 24:7

- Ezekiel 36:26

• Psalm 37:4 (NLT)

DIGGING DEEPER

In the story of the loaves and the fishes, Jesus was able to take the small offering, the humble offering, of a boy's lunch and multiply it, expand it, and use it to meet the needs of thousands of people. Looking at your own heart, soul, mind, and strength, do you see things God might be able to use if you were to put them in His hands? What are they?

PONDER & PRAY

There may be times when we doubt that God could notice, even need us for His plans. We can't help but wonder what He sees in us, what use we could possibly be, what good we can do. But God is able to use what is given wholly to Him. Pray this week for the desire to live wholeheartedly for God. Give Him your heart, soul, mind, and strength. He can take your simplest gift and multiply it greatly for His glory.

TRINKETS TO TREASURE

The Lord calls to each of us. Don't shuffle your feet off in a corner and mumble, "Who me?" We may not feel our lives can offer much to the Lord's grand scheme, but that doesn't matter. The trinket for this lesson is a loaf of bread. It may not seem like much to us, but our humble loaf of cherry nut bread may just be the loaf of bread He breaks apart to feed five thousand souls.

NOTES & PRAYER REQUESTS

NOTES & PRAYER REQUESTS

CHAPTER FIVE

THE FEAR FACTOR

"ACCORDING TO THE PURPOSE OF HIM WHO WORKS ALL THINGS ACCORDING TO THE COUNSEL OF HIS WILL."

Ephesians 1:11 NKJV

*I*f there's one thing that stands in the way of giving our all to God, it's probably fear. Who of us hasn't wondered, "If I surrender my will, my life to God, what would He do with it?" Faced with the loss of control over our futures, it's no wonder some of us get a little balky. After all, look at the track record of the men and women who put their lives wholly in the Lord's hands.

Abraham was asked to give up that which was most precious to him—his son. Moses, though he was shy, was pushed into the spotlight of public speaking. Joseph had his reputation torn to shreds and went to prison on false charges. David found himself face to face with a giant in a do-or-die situation. Daniel was conspired against by jealous peers and wound up being thrown to the lions. Admittedly, all their stories turned out okay in the end, but would *you* want to live through them?

CLEARING ⊀ THE ⊁ COBWEBS

What kinds of games did you play at slumber parties when you were a girl?

We may all agree that with God, all things are possible, but which of us wants to volunteer to do the impossible? If we give our life into God's hands, before we know it, we might be standing in line at the passport office, updating our shots and enrolling in total emersion language courses, bound for who knows where! What are you afraid God might ask you to give up? What are you afraid God might ask you to do?

1. God's scope is tremendous. His perspective is vastly different from our own simply because God sees and knows all things! And why not? After all, He made all things!

- What does John 1:3 tell us about creation?

- What does Acts 17:25 say that God gives to us?

- What are Paul's memorable words in Romans 11:36?

• Why does Colossians 1:16 say that all things were created?

2. Not only did God *create* all things, Scripture says that God can *do* all the things He wishes to do. How does Jesus put it in Matthew 19:26?

> *"Have you ever said something that you weren't proud of? At least forty people in my Sunday school class heard me say more than once, 'I just can't totally commit myself to the Lord, because He might send me to Africa, and I don't like flies!'"*
>
> Thelma Wells

3. According to Scripture, with God "all things" are possible. But that's a wide-open field of unknown things for us, and many of us find that just a little frightening. But let's take a look at some more of the things that are a part of that "all."

___1 Chronicles 29:14   a. "I am the LORD, who makes all things."

___Psalm 57:2   b. The Spirit is able to teach us all things.

___Isaiah 44:24   c. All things exist by God's will.

___Luke 21:22   d. All things come from God.

___John 14:26   e. All things are by and for the Lord.

___Hebrews 1:3   f. All things that were written will be fulfilled.

___Hebrews 2:10   g. God is able to perform all things for me.

___Revelation 4:11   h. The Lord upholds all things by His word.

4. The enormity of many of those statements is really mind-boggling. We cannot comprehend the vastness of God's power. But some of those "all things" verses get pretty personal. Some of the "all things" verses are downright encouraging!

• According to Romans 8:32, what does Paul say God freely gives to us?

• What is the wonderful promise in Philippians 4:13?

• What vital things does Peter say are ours in 2 Peter 1:3?

5. What is the "all things" promise of Romans 8:28?

*H*ave you ever been to a girls' slumber party and been the unlucky participant in a game of Truth or Dare? In this game, you find yourself at the mercy of your friends, forced to give up your most closely kept secrets or do the most outrageous stunts. These silly feats are something to giggle over if you're a tweener, up past your bedtime. But what if you're a grown woman, and you feel like you're in a game of Truth or Dare with God? Can we trust Him with our secrets? What unforeseeable task might He ask us to do?

6. God may promise that all things work together for good and that all things work together according to His purpose, but that doesn't always feel like enough. We'd like a vote, or at least veto power in the process! What does Ephesians 1:11–12 tell us about how God works?

7. God may just choose to do the impossible in our lives, whether we're looking for it or not! He's working according to His own plans and purposes. But what does 1 Peter 4:11 tell *us* to do in all the things we say and do?

> "There resides in the heart of every believer a little pocket of fear. For some of us it's cowardice. For others, it's timidity. Although we know the Savior gives courage and power, sometimes we feel safer in our little pocket than in His big provision."
>
> Luci Swindoll

8. We're not promised a peek at life from God's perspective. Often, we don't understand what in the world God is doing. We have to trust that God is working for good and for His own glory. What He *does* promise is hindsight!

- What was Joseph's unique perspective in Genesis 50:20?

- What did Isaiah see clearly after all his suffering, according to Isaiah 38:17?

- What words did Paul use to encourage the brethren in Philippians 1:12?

> "That's the thing about most of my personal victories: They're characterized by knee-knocking fear amidst God's empowering strength."
>
> Patsy Clairmont

9. My brother-in-law, a former marine, is fond of saying, "What doesn't kill you only makes you stronger." Giving God our all is not and never will be an easy thing to do. But we must set aside our fears and trust that God's good will be shiningly apparent in hindsight one day. Do you still have fears? Share them honestly with the Lord here.

DIGGING DEEPER

Looking back at his life, Paul was able to see God's hand. Circumstances didn't matter to him, because he knew God was at work whether things seemed to be going well or going badly. He was able to say, "I know how to live on almost nothing or with everything. I have learned the secret of living in every situation, whether it is with a full stomach or empty, with plenty or little" (Phil. 4:12 NLT). In "all things" (NKJV), Paul had learned to be content. Looking back, can you see God's hand in your life, working things out for good? Looking forward, do you find yourself disposed to trust Him, even though the path may seem uncertain?

PONDER & PRAY

Many of us hang back from giving God our all because we're afraid of what He might ask of us. Fear blocks our way, and so we must deal with it honestly. This week, talk over your fears with the Lord. Tell Him what's in your heart. Tell Him what hinders you.

TRINKETS TO TREASURE

With God, all things are possible, but few of us would willingly sign up for mission impossible. We admire the lives of saints who had their faith tried and triumphed, but we're not willing to put ourselves in their shoes. We think putting our lives in God's hands might end us up somewhere we don't want to be. So our trinket this week is a passport—a sure sign that God might just ship us out of our comfort zones.

NOTES & PRAYER REQUESTS

_____

_____

_____

_____

_____

CHAPTER SIX

Do You Trust Me?

*"But as for me, I trust in You, O Lord; I say,
'You are my God.'"*

Psalm 31:14 NKJV

or weeks now, I've been telling my daughters that I'd buy them a trundle bed. I explained to them what a trundle bed was, how it worked, and how much space it would save in their little bedroom. Then, recently, we were in a department store where a few beds were lined up. The girls got all excited, hoping to see a trundle bed "in person." Sure enough, they had one.

The only trouble was, the bed didn't match up with what one of my daughters thought a trundle bed should be. "That's not a trundle bed," she stated flatly. "Yes, it is," stated her older and wiser mother. "Well, I really don't think so," persisted the child. "Look," I said, "See the drawer underneath. You can even see the mattress peeking out. It rolls out to make a bed. That's what a trundle bed is." "But it's not . . ." By this time, we were rescued from further escalation by a sweet sales associate. I couldn't get over the sheer audacity of my daughter's refusal to believe me. I know what

Clearing ↗ the ↖ Cobwebs

Have you ever had to take someone's word for something?

a trundle bed is, and that was a trundle bed. But my child was so sure that she knew best.

Is that so different from us? God tells us, "This is what I have planned for you." But we look at our lot and say, "This is not what I had in mind." "I know you better than you know yourself, child. This is what you need right now. Trust me, I know." And still, we shake our heads, "But it's not . . ." Faced with disappointed expectations, we have the audacity not to believe God.

1. Believing in God and believing God are such integral parts of the Christian life that we are often simply called "believers."

* What does Jesus ask His followers to believe in, according to John 14:1?

* According to John 20:31, what helps our belief and what does that belief bring us?

- What does Paul say God's Word does for believers in 1 Thessalonians 2:13?

2. There is believing, and then there is *believing*. Anyone can acknowledge that there is a God. We're not alone there. "You believe that there is one God. You do well. Even the demons believe—and tremble!" (James 2:19 NKJV). What does Psalm 9:10 say the people do, beyond just knowing God's name?

> *"I'm so grateful Jesus enables me to change, one groaning effort at a time, and I'm thankful for those folks in my life who have given me the space and time to change."*
>
> **Patsy Clairmont**

3. And what was David's proclamation in Psalm 31:14?

4. This is a message that cannot be repeated often enough. God repeats it over and over and over in Scripture. Can't you hear His voice? "Trust Me, trust Me, trust Me!" Each of these verses gives us ways how and reasons to trust God. Sum up their messages.

- Psalm 62:8

- Psalm 20:7

- Psalm 36:7

- Psalm 52:8

- Psalm 64:10

- Psalm 71:5

• Psalm 73:28

• Proverbs 3:5

• Isaiah 12:2

5. Just look at the promises He makes to those who are willing to trust.

___ Psalm 16:1   a. Those who trust find God their rock and fortress.

___ Psalm 18:2   b. Those who trust in God won't be condemned.

___ Psalm 18:30   c. The man who makes the LORD his trust is blessed.

___ Psalm 34:22   d. Those who trust in God cannot be moved.

___ Psalm 37:3   e. God preserves those who trust Him.

___ Psalm 40:4   f. Those who trust in God have nothing to fear.

___ Psalm 56:4   g. God is a shield to all who trust in Him.

___ Psalm 125:1   h. Those who trust can feed on God's faith-fulness.

hy is it so hard to take someone else's word for something? Even when we know our elders have our best interest in mind, wise counsel can be hard to swallow. We prefer to see for ourselves what the consequences of our actions will be. Oh, I'm all for learning by trial and error in some things. As Ms. Frizzle of Magic School Bus fame would say, "Take chances! Make mistakes! Get messy!" But Scripture praises those who are teachable. When we take God's word for it, and believe what He's promised, and live as if we did—that's trusting!

6. What does Nahum 1:7 say that God knows?

7. What does Psalm 34:8 invite us to do?

"Be anxious for nothing. Why shouldn't we worry about it? Because worry says to God, 'Lord, I don't trust You.'"

Thelma Wells

8. What does David urge us to do in Psalm 37:5?

DIGGING DEEPER

There's a vast chasm between believing there *is* a God and believing *in* God. Mental assent is not sufficient for salvation. Faith must be involved. In the Gospel of John, trusting God is often spoken of as believing God. Look at these verses, which speak of a believing faith.

- John 3:36

- John 6:29

- John 11:26

- John 11:27

- John 11:40

PONDER & PRAY

Do you trust God? This week, ponder this. Do you believe what God has said? Do you trust Him with all your heart? How far will you trust Him? With what will you trust Him? Pray that the Spirit will help you honestly assess your ability to trust. Seek out the Scriptures, which can build your trust. Believe God and His promises for you. Taste and see—give Him a try—and let God prove Himself faithful in your life.

TRINKETS TO TREASURE

This week's trinket is a reminder of God's faithfulness—a shield. The psalms often promise that God will be a shield to those who trust in Him. This week's lesson challenges us to place our trust in God, believe in Him, and live as if we did so.

NOTES & PRAYER REQUESTS

CHAPTER SEVEN

PUTTING IT IN GOD'S HANDS . . .

"CASTING ALL YOUR CARE UPON HIM, FOR HE CARES FOR YOU"

1 Peter 5:7 NKJV

o you know a backseat driver? (You may be one!) These dear folks are quite certain that those in the driver's seat are completely unaware of the rules of the road. So, they take it upon themselves to direct their designated driver through traffic. Or perhaps you've driven with a panicky passenger before? These are the ones who ride with a white-knuckle grip on their armrests. It doesn't take much to evoke little gasps of fear from them—changing traffic lights, the sight of brake lights ahead, low-flying birds. If you drive too fast for their comfort level, they'll start spasmodically reaching for a non-existent brake pedal. Freeways make them tense, and passing semi trucks bring on moans of horror and prayers for mercy.

How do you take to God's place in the driver's seat of your life? Are you still trying to dictate

CLEARING ↗ THE ↖ COBWEBS

What's the heaviest load you've ever had to carry?

the route? Are you criticizing His technique? Or maybe you're more like the panicky passenger, not quite trusting the driver to get you safely to your destination?

1. For many believers, especially women, "submit" is a bad word. Bring it up in any discussion and you've opened up a can of worms. When we say we want to give God our all, aren't we saying we want to submit to Him in every area of our lives?

- What do the pretenders of Psalm 81:15 do?

- What does James tell us to do in James 4:7?

- What are Jesus' words of ultimate submission in Luke 22:42?

2. When we allow Jesus to be the Lord of our lives, there are certain "perks" that come with putting ourselves into His hands. What is the one we find in 1 Peter 5:7?

3. How many of us persist in trying to make our own way in life, fending for ourselves? We limp along like Christian in *Pilgrim's Progress*, with our burden strapped to our back. How does Isaiah 1:4 (NLT) describe such a people?

> "As you walk through your days, you encounter various situations in life that trouble you. If you're like me, there are decisions that must be made that seem bigger than I have the capacity to handle."
>
> Luci Swindoll

4. What kind of burdens do we end up trying to carry on our own?

___ Exodus 6:9	a. The burden of a guilty conscience
___ Exodus 18:18	b. The burden of guilt
___ 1 Samuel 25:31	c. The burden of dread for what is to come
___ Psalm 38:4	d. The burden of becoming overworked
___ Psalm 66:11	e. The burden of fear of abandonment
___ Isaiah 26:16	f. The burden of enslavement
___ Jeremiah 23:33	g. The burden of discouragement
___ Matthew 23:4	h. The burden of religious disciplines
___ Luke 12:50	i. The burden of God's discipline

5. What does the Lord give relief from in Psalm 81:6 (NLT)?

"Starting with every piece of us—all that is lovely, hideous, fun, dry, sinful, beautiful—we surrender it to God. We allow the hard things we go through to make us better rather than bitter."

Nicole Johnson

6. What does Jesus tell us of burdens in Matthew 11:30?

I like the picture of our putting ourselves into God's hands. Have you heard Kathy Troccoli sing her song, "My Life Is In Your Hands"? It's a beautiful depiction of a believer's heart of trust as she gives her all to God. Look at some of the lyrics. "Life can be so good; / Life can be so hard. /Never knowing what each day/ Will bring to where you are." Or how about "Nothing is for sure; /Nothing is for keeps." Life is filled with ups and downs and all kinds of uncertainties. But look at the chorus:

My life is in Your hands.
My heart is in Your keeping.
I'm never without hope,
Not when my future is with You.
My life is in Your hands,
And though I may not see clearly,
I will lift my voice and sing,
Cause Your love does amazing things.
Lord, I know, my life is in Your hands.

When we find our hearts willing to give God our all, and we put our lives into His hands, we make a wonderful discovery. When we give up resisting and give God our all, we give up our burdens as well. All those fears and worries and sad memories and sufferings. All the overwhelming odds, the discouragement, the stress, and the guilt. He carries them now.

7. Not only does God carry our burdens, He carries us!

- What does Deuteronomy 1:31 compare God's care for His people with?

- What does God do for those who belong to Him, according to Isaiah 40:11?

- How long does God carry us, according to Isaiah 46:4?

8. What else is God willing to bear for us, according to Isaiah 53:4?

9. What does Psalm 28:9 invite God to do for us, His own people?

> *"Each of us has something broken in our lives: a broken promise, a broken dream, a broken marriage, a broken heart . . . and we must decide how we're going to deal with our brokenness."*
>
> Luci Swindoll

DIGGING DEEPER

Some Scriptures speak of God carrying us in His arms. What a beautiful picture of His love and care. Here are two more passages that speak of this.

- Psalm 68:19

- Isaiah 63:9

PONDER & PRAY

Consider, for a moment, the delicate balance of God's lordship over our lives. On the one hand, we are put in a position of submitting our will to God's. But on the other hand God takes care of those who belong to Him. This week, pray for insights into the blessings that are yours because you have placed your life in God's hands. Ask God to show you those times in your life when He's carried you. Pray for His gentle shepherding of your heart to continue.

TRINKETS TO TREASURE

Your trinket this week is a silly little thing—a bobber. Fishermen use them on their lines as they cast for fish. For you, the bobber also stands for casting. We belong to God and put our lives in His hands. That means that we can cast all our burdens, our cares, our fears, and our sorrows onto Him. We cast them away, but we must also remember we're not meant to reel them back in again!

NOTES & PRAYER REQUESTS

CHAPTER EIGHT

...AND LEAVING IT THERE

"THE WAY OF LIFE WINDS UPWARD FOR THE WISE."

Proverbs 15:24 NKJV

I come from a long line of pack-rats. The old farmhouse I grew up in was packrat heaven. We had a closet in every bedroom, floor-to-ceiling cupboards in three rooms, a linen closet, a cedar closet, pantry shelves, a full basement, and a root cellar. And that was just inside! There was also a chicken coop, machine shed, utility shed, and a huge empty dairy barn with two silos. There was no lack of space for all the stuff. Now most packrats are frugal people. They can't bear to let go of something that might come in handy at a later date. You never know what you might regret getting rid of! To a pack-rat, cleaning out really just means rearranging the stuff.

Far too often, in our spiritual lives, we find our packrat nature creeping in. We latch onto God's promises that we can cast all our cares upon Him and that He will bear all our griefs and sorrows, but we're strangely reluctant to let go of

CLEARING ↗ THE ↖ COBWEBS

Do you have something that you never really use, but you could never, ever part with?

our burdens! For whatever reason, some of us have a hard time with this. We give Him our worries and fears only to pluck them up again. We've just about settled a matter of the heart only to find it stirred up again. We long to give Him our life and put ourselves completely in His hands only to seize control again. Putting things into God's hands is one thing. But leaving them there is another.

1. There are times when I wish we could give things to God in the same way He forgives the things we confess.

- What does Psalm 103:12 tell us about the forgiveness of God?

- How does Isaiah 38:17 picture God's disposal of our sins?

- What does God promise us in Jeremiah 31:34?

2. It would be nice to give God our all and know that it would stay that way, but we have such a tendency to take things back. This pattern was prominent in Israel's history. At times, they would live in vibrant fellowship with the Lord, but then they would slip back into sinful ways. What does Hosea 11:7 call this activity?

> *"There are times when oh, what we wouldn't give for a little direction. Desperately we long for God's guidance. How many times have I heard people say, 'I really want to do what God wants me to do, but what is it?'"*
>
> Luci Swindoll

3. Backsliding—sliding back into our old way of doing things. We take one step forward only to take two steps back. This is the vicious cycle we have all experienced.

___ Isaiah 57:17   a. "Return . . . and I will heal your back-slidings."

___ Jeremiah 3:6   b. "He went on backsliding in the way of his heart."

___ Jeremiah 3:22   c. "I will heal their backsliding, I will love them freely."

___ Jeremiah 8:5   d. "How long will you gad about, backsliding daughter?"

___ Jeremiah 31:22   e. "Have you seen what backsliding Israel has done?"

___ Hosea 14:4   f. "Why has this people slidden back perpetually?"

4. God is able to do so much more than we are able. What does Psalm 132:11 (NLT) say about God and His words?

> "God speaks to us clearly. He means what He says. When He says He'll provide, we can count on that. When He promises peace, wisdom, strength, or comfort, they are ours. God imparts His word and keeps it."
>
> Luci Swindoll

5. Not only are we guilty of taking back our promises, we sometimes can't help looking back at what we've had to leave behind. What does Luke 9:62 say about looking back?

o you remember Lot's wife? Jesus wants us to! "Remember Lot's wife" (Luke 17:32 NKJV). Here was a lady we can understand. She loved her husband. She loved her daughters. She loved her home. Though they'd lived as nomads for many years, Lot had finally been coaxed back into civilization. No more nomadic tents among the herds for Lot's wife! She had a real home on a quiet cul-de-sac, with the cutest little courtyard and just a short walk from the bazaar. What bliss! Lot was a man of some wealth and influence in their community, so Lot's wife lacked for nothing. She knew all the right people, shopped in all the best stores, fussed over her hair and robes, and delighted in throwing dinner parties. As far as Lot's wife was concerned, they'd "arrived."

But then God said it was time to leave it all behind. "Head for the hills and don't look back!" Lot's wife was sick at heart. She didn't want to leave her home behind. She didn't want to give up the comforts she'd grown accustomed to. She dragged her feet, she dreaded her future, and so she disobeyed. Lot's wife looked back, and in doing so she sealed her fate. "But his wife looked back behind him, and she became a pillar of salt" (Gen. 19:26 NKJV).

6. There's a line in the great hymn "Come Thou Fount of Every Blessing," which says, "Prone to wander, Lord I feel it. Prone to leave the God I love." Sin and self pull at us all the time. What rather unsavory comparison does Solomon make in Proverbs 26:11 about those who don't learn from their mistakes?

7♦ We wander. We make mistakes. We stumble along the way. But if we're honest, we'd admit we knew better. What is Peter's addition to Solomon's pithy proverb in 2 Peter 2:22?

"In the New Testament we are called to be living sacrifices. That's in contrast to the dead sacrifices of the Old Testament, where a young animal would be killed. A slain animal no longer has a choice, but you and I do. Think about it: A living sacrifice can crawl back off the altar if it gets too hot. It requires a daily choice to stay on that altar no matter how intense the heat."

Sheila Walsh

8♦ There's a reason our spiritual lives are often called our "walk." There's always a danger of wandering off the path, of sliding backwards, of stumbling over some obstacle. But there's also a picture of following in the Lord's footsteps, of pressing on, climbing higher. How does Proverbs 15:24 put it?

9. What is the prayer of Psalm 119:37?

DIGGING DEEPER

God invites us to put things into His very capable hands. Here are a few
more verses that talk about God's hands and the things He's willing to
hold.

- Exodus 18:19

- Ecclesiastes 9:1

- Luke 23:46

- 1 Peter 5:6

PONDER & PRAY

This week's prayer might find you putting a few things back in the Lord's
hands that you thought were there, but have mysteriously found their way
into the backs of your hearts and minds. Giving things to God is hard
enough, but leaving things with God is trickier still. Ask the Lord to help
you be honest with Him and with yourself.

TRINKETS TO TREASURE

Too often we try to hoard things we don't need, "just in case." We hang on to things that are better let go. The trinket for this week is a packrat, who can remind us not to cling to things God can carry for us. He's welcomed us to cast our cares onto Him. He's offered to bear our sorrows. Now, we are trying to give Him our all! It's no use trying to keep all these things. And when we let things go, we shouldn't go rummaging back around for them again.

NOTES & PRAYER REQUESTS

CHAPTER NINE

IT'S TOO HARD!

"NO MATTER WHICH WAY I TURN, I CAN'T MAKE MYSELF DO RIGHT. I WANT TO, BUT I CAN'T."

Romans 7:18 NLT

When I was of the proper age, my parents enrolled me in piano lessons. I think my mother had visions of beautiful music drifting out of the living room someday. Our piano was certainly beautiful, but the music I made was not. Now my own children are of an age to begin piano lessons.

We inherited Grandma's piano, and I began having visions of beautiful music drifting out of my living room. But my children began asking me some very uncomfortable questions. "Did you take piano lessons, Mama?" I admitted that I had. "Can you play piano for us?" I admitted that I couldn't. "Why not?" I admitted that I could not play. "Why not?" And I had to admit to my children that when I was their age, I didn't like to practice the piano and had given it up. It wasn't long before those wily youngsters were threatening to give up. With tears of frustration, they'd come to me and say they'd like to quit. "It's too hard!"

CLEARING THE COBWEBS

Have you ever tried something new, only to be completely discouraged because you had so much trouble with it? Have you ever stuck with something that was hard to do and felt the joy of finally mastering it?

Feeling I'd better rectify the example I had set, I found a book of beautiful, but fairly simple classical piano pieces and took my turn every day in the living room. It was painful. I inched through the music note by note, chord by chord. I couldn't get my left hand to keep in step with my right hand. The tempo was off and I felt fumble-fingered. The kids cheerfully watched me make mistake after mistake. They'd call encouragement from the kitchen: "That's okay Mama. I think you're getting better!" But after a week of dogged practice, I could play the first line through. And after a month, I could play the first half. It took three months for me to master the piece, and I still miss a note now and then, but I'm glad I didn't give up.

"Some women have it tough. They've weathered mega obstacles with grace and integrity. Their fortitude reminds me of the bulbs I planted in my yard last fall. They lay dormant through the bitter winter, but then in the spring they began the arduous journey of pushing up life through the crusty earth while sending stabilizing roots into the soil."

Patsy Clairmont

1. If something is important to us, if we really want something badly, we find a way to make it happen. Piano lessons, pin tucks, pie crusts, portraits, pirouettes—they all take practice! But some things are beyond our control. Take, for instance, Paul's words in Romans 7:18. What did he say he simply couldn't do?

2. Is it a relief to know that even Paul—Paul the missionary evangelist, the apostle, the writer of our Scriptures—didn't always get it right? Still, Paul never used this as an excuse to give up. In fact, what did he urge believers to do in 1 Thessalonians 5:15?

3. If we look at it one way, pursuing something doesn't necessarily mean we'll ever catch up with it (at least on this side of heaven), but our lives will reflect the effort we make, and Scripture tells us this is good.

___ Psalm 34:14	a. The sinner's heart pursues its own gain.
___ Ezekiel 33:31	b. Seek peace and pursue it.
___ Romans 14:19	c. Pursue righteousness, godliness, faith…
___ 1 Corinthians 14:1	d. Pursue faith, love, and peace with the brethren.
___ 1 Timothy 6:11	e. Seek peace and pursue it.
___ 2 Timothy 2:22	f. Pursue love and spiritual gifts.
___ Hebrews 12:14	g. Pursue peace and holiness.
___ 1 Peter 3:11	h. Pursue the things which make for peace and edify.

4. There are days when we'd like to sit right down, throw back our head, and wail, "It's too hard!" Well, in many ways, the Christian walk *is* hard. Just keep in mind, nobody said it would be easy. They just said it would be worth it. Consider each of these paraphrases of Scripture verses. Each passage talks about our tendency to want things to be easy and the simple fact that things aren't. See if you can recognize each verse and assign it a reference. You're looking at Acts 14:22, Romans 15:3, 1 Corinthians 7:35, Philippians 3:18–19, and 1 Thessalonians 5:3—though not necessarily in that order!

> *"That's exactly what Jesus did. He didn't make it easy for himself by avoiding people's troubles, but waded right in and helped out. 'I took on the troubles of the troubled,' is the way Scripture puts it"* (MSG).

Reference: _____

> *"There are many out there taking other paths, choosing other goals, and trying to get you to go along with them. I've warned you of them many times; sadly, I'm having to do it again. All they want is easy street. They hate Christ's Cross. But easy street is a dead-end street. Those who live there make their bellies their gods; belches are their praise; all they can think of is their appetites"* (MSG).

Reference: _____

"Putting muscle and sinew in the lives of the disciples, urging them to stick with what they had begun to believe and not quit, making it clear to them that it wouldn't be easy: 'Anyone signing up for the kingdom of God has to go through plenty of hard times'" (MSG).

Reference: _____

"About the time everybody's walking around complacently, congratulating each other — 'We've sure got it made! Now we can take it easy!' — suddenly everything will fall apart" (MSG).

Reference: _____

"I'm trying to be helpful and make it as easy as possible for you, not make things harder. All I want is for you to be able to develop a way of life in which you can spend plenty of time together with the Master without a lot of distractions" (MSG).

Reference: _____

5. As a matter of fact, Scripture has far more to say about enduring than about everything being easy!

- What does Matthew 24:13 have to say about those who endure?

- According to 1 Corinthians 3:14, who will be rewarded?

- What does Paul tell us to do in 2 Timothy 2:3?

- What amazing promise does Paul share with us in 2 Timothy 2:12?

- According to James 5:11, how are those who endure described?

*H*ave you ever watched a baby chick hatch? We had an incubator in our dining room one spring, and watched nearly thirty hatchlings make their way out of their shells. One minute there's a damp creature sprawled uncertainly on the newspaper, and the next there's a fuzzy baby chick running around, drinking water, and pecking at the feed trays. The transformation is amazingly fast. Chickens have babies who are able to run about and find their own food within minutes of hatching.

I think we often expect to make those kinds of leaps in our spiritual lives. We want to grow up quickly. We want to be wise. We want to be mature. We want to be able to face hard times with patient endurance. But in reality, we're much slower to learn. We can't take off running until we've first learned to crawl, and then take tottering steps. Baby steps. Our faith is growing, but it takes time to gain strength. Don't be discouraged by those times when it seems too hard. Those are growing pains.

6. What prevents endurance in Jesus' parable found in Matthew 13:21?

7. The key to enduring through hard times seems to be roots! Roots anchor. Roots draw strength. Roots support the bearing of good fruit. What should we be rooted in according to Ephesians 3:17?

8. What is Paul's little reminder to us in Romans 11:18?

> "Growth and change are synonymous. Perhaps you're in the midst of change, and it feels threatening. That's often the initial signal that alerts us to a season of growth."
>
> Patsy Clairmont

9. Send down your roots into God's strength. He will supply what is needed when times are hard. Look at the promises each of these proverbs holds for those whose root is righteous:

- Proverbs 12:3

- Proverbs 12:12

> *"God never calls without enabling us. In other words, if He calls you to do something, He makes it possible for you to do it."*
>
> Luci Swindoll

DIGGING DEEPER

Did you know that *Root* is one of the names of Christ? Take a look!

- Isaiah 11:10

- Isaiah 53:2

- Romans 15:12

PONDER & PRAY

Have you had the kind of week that leaves you throwing your head back, screaming, "It's too hard!"? Then tell the Lord so! He listens with a patience unknown to mankind. Pour it all out to Him, but then ask the Lord to make this a growing time for you. Stretch your roots a little deeper into His strength. Stretch your faith a little further than it was willing to go before. Pray for the willingness to persevere.

TRINKETS TO TREASURE

Our faith is growing, but there will still be times when it all seems "too hard." We need time to send down deep roots. We need to learn how to trust, to gain strength, to depend on the Lord. So we take baby steps along our spiritual path. Your trinket this week is a pair of baby booties. They'll remind you that faith grows during the hard times, so don't be discouraged by these growing pains.

NOTES & PRAYER REQUESTS

_____

_____

_____

_____

CHAPTER TEN

As Good as
His Word

"GOD, WHO CANNOT LIE."

Titus 1:2 NKJV

Are you familiar with impulse racks? They're the displays of odds and ends that stores place next to the checkout counters, hoping you'll pick up something on impulse and add it to your cart. Last year I found the cutest little thing. Our local hardware store had a bucket full of tiny little levels, no bigger than a couple inches long, attached to key rings. Now Christmas was getting close, so I picked one up, figuring it would be a perfect stocking stuffer for my difficult-to-shop-for husband. And that little doo-dad *was* a big hit—with my seven-year-old. He commandeered the thing and began methodically checking the level of every tabletop and windowsill throughout the house. He reported in periodically, letting us know we weren't in danger of tipping over any time soon.

CLEARING
THE
COBWEBS

What is the strangest item on the impulse racks at the checkout counter that you suddenly realized you couldn't live without?

Of course, we didn't always live on the level. When my husband and I were first married, we rented a house that was slightly out of kilter. It was one of those charming old houses that had seen better days. It had aged gracefully and settled itself comfortably on its foundations, but there wasn't a level board left in it. The kitchen had a distinctive downhill slope towards the basement door. The plaster walls had some wobble in them. Whenever we were hanging pictures, we had to decide if they should be straight in relation to the ceiling, the floor, or the line of a nearby window or doorframe.

It's far too easy for our lives to be knocked out of kilter. When we use our limited perspective to try to square things up, it's surprising how far off we can be. When we're using sloping floorboards and slanting ceilings as guides, we've not much hope of finding a straight line. That's why we need to look beyond ourselves, beyond our surroundings. We need to find the horizon line. We need to look at One who's straight and true. We need to find the Level.

1. When someone is telling the truth, we'll often say, "He's on the level." Think about what you know of God. Do these descriptions apply?

- ❑ Promise keeper
- ❑ Honest as the day is long
- ❑ Straight shooter
- ❑ True blue
- ❑ On the level
- ❑ Tried and true
- ❑ Walks the talk

- ❑ Aboveboard
- ❑ Up-front
- ❑ Plain-spoken
- ❑ Dyed in the wool
- ❑ Straight as an arrow
- ❑ Square
- ❑ Rock solid

2. You cannot give yourself over to someone you do not trust, and you cannot trust someone you do not know. So how do we know we can trust God? We start by finding out all we can about Him. What do these verses tell us?

Deuteronomy 4:31 — God is...

Psalm 68:20 — God is...

John 3:33 — God is...

John 4:24 — God is...

> "Life is treacherous, and life is tremendous. We all know this, but here is the clincher: The stabilizing truth that acts as a cohesive to hold us together is that, through all life's weather patterns, God is good."
>
> **Patsy Clairmont**

1 Corinthians 1:9 — God is...

1 John 1:5 — God is...

1 John 4:16 — God is...

3. The writers of Scripture searched for words to describe the Lord. He was beyond description, but by drawing comparisons they conveyed their impressions of the Divine to us.

- To what is God compared in Deuteronomy 4:24?

- What does David call God in Psalm 46:1?

- In Psalm 47:7, what is God called?

- How does Psalm 84:11 describe the Lord God?

4. God is a father to us. He is a husband to the widow. He is a gentle shepherd to the weary. Jesus is the Bread of Life, the Living Water, the Way, the Truth, and the Life, and the very Beginning and End of all things!

Deuteronomy 10:17 — "For the Lord your God is _____ of _____ and _____ of _____, the _____ God, _____ and _____, who shows no _____" (NKJV).

Joshua 1:9 — "Be _____ and of good _____; do not be _____, nor be _____, for the Lord your God is _____ you _____ you go" (NKJV).

Job 36:22 — "Behold, God is _____ by His _____; Who _____ like Him?" (NKJV).

5. Each verse we uncover reveals some new facet of God's personality and perfection.

___ Deuteronomy 20:4   a. Our God is greater than all gods.

___ 2 Chronicles 2:5   b. God is good to those who are pure in heart.

___ 2 Chronicles 30:9   c. God makes all grace abound to you.

___ Job 9:4   d. God is the author of peace.

___ Psalm 73:1   e. God is not ashamed to be called our God.

___ Romans 14:4   f. God is He who goes with you. He fights for you.

___ 1 Corinthians 14:33   g. God is well pleased when we do good and
                              share.

___ 2 Corinthians 9:8   h. The LORD your God is gracious and
                             merciful.

___ Hebrews 6:10   i. God is wise in heart and mighty in
                             strength.

___ Hebrews 11:16   j. God sees all the work you do in His name.

___ Hebrews 13:16   k. God is able to make us stand.

6. We often speak of having a personal relationship with God. David spoke of the Lord with great intimacy. He called the Lord God, *my* God.

2 Samuel 22:33 — God is my…

Psalm 54:4 — God is my…

Psalm 73:26 — God is my…

Psalm 59:17 — God is my…

Psalms 62:7 — God is my...

Psalm 74:12 — God is my...

7. For all we know of God, can our infinite minds really grasp all that God is? What is Job's opinion on the matter in Job 36:26?

8. With all these inestimable qualities, do you still find yourself reluctant to place yourself into God's hands? All right, then consider what we learn of God in 1 Corinthians 1:25. What do we learn of Him there?

> *"When daily living plagues you with questions about what God is up to in your life, recall how He has made Himself known to you in the past. Thank Him for drawing you to believe in Him through these experiences. Allow them to restore your confidence in the God who never changes."*
>
> Thelma Wells

> *"Christ offers you all that you need and more; it's up to you to receive it and then to live as those who believe it."*
>
> Patsy Clairmont

9. There is one last point to make in this lesson. What does Ezra 8:22 say about God's purposes for those who seek Him?

DIGGING DEEPER

We have spent most of the lesson looking at what our Bible says God is. Let's spend a little extra time in discovering who God says, "I am…"

Isaiah 42:8
Isaiah 43:15
Isaiah 44:6
John 6:35
John 8:12
John 10:9
John 10:11
John 11:25
John 14:6
John 15:5
Revelation 1:8
Revelation 22:16

Ponder & Pray

As you go through this week, ponder through this amazing selection of verses. They tell us so many details about God, and yet we're only receiving a glimpse! Pray for an appreciation of just Who God is. Bolster your conviction with the facts! Ask the Lord to help you grasp just how much and how far you can trust Him. Pray for confident assurance that God is as good as His word in all things, even your own life.

Trinkets to Treasure

You cannot give yourself into the hands of one you do not trust, and you cannot trust one you do not know, so make it a point to get to know God through His Word. God is as good as His word. He's true blue. He's a straight shooter. He's on the level. So this week's trinket is one of those handy little levels. We use them to keep things squared up around the house. We can use this little gadget to remind us to keep our lives squared up with God. His promises to us are true. His character is unchanging. So we should live with our lives lined up to His Word.

Notes & Prayer Requests

CHAPTER ELEVEN

SURRENDERED

"PRESENT YOURSELVES TO GOD AS BEING ALIVE FROM THE DEAD, AND YOUR MEMBERS AS INSTRUMENTS OF RIGHTEOUSNESS TO GOD."

Romans 6:13 NKJV

I suppose in recent years *sur-render* has become a rather outmoded term. When we think of surrender, we think of battles lost and of arrests made. "Put your hands up!" "Reach for the sky!" "Keep your hands where I can see 'em!" But surrender does crop up in some of our favorite old hymns. The most famous is probably "I Surrender All."

> *All to Jesus I surrender; All*
> *to Him I freely give;*
> *I will ever love and trust Him,*
> *in His presence daily live.*

> *refrain:*
> *I surrender all, I surrender all,*
> *All to Thee, my blessed Savior,*
> *I surrender all.*

CLEARING ✈ THE ☚ COBWEBS

Has there ever been a time when you would have liked to wave the white flag of surrender and give up?

What does *surrender* mean? According to the dictionary, surrender means relinquishing control to another. It means we're done fighting. We're giving up. We've stopped struggling. We've laid down our weapons. We've acknowledged another's authority. We've given up our own rights. We've put ourselves at another's mercy. It means we're willing to follow another's orders.

1. It's a trite little platitude: "Let go and let God." Easy to say, difficult to do. It's not any easier than Paul's admonition from Romans 12:1:

I _____ you therefore, _____, (I urge you, fellow believers)

By the _____ of God, (with the Lord's own help)

That you _____ your _____ (give God your all)

A _____ _____, (the everyday you and all your days)

_____, _____ to God, (set apart for Him, pleasing Him)

Which is your _____ _____. (it's not too much to ask!)

2. Most of the early Christians had grown up in Jewish homes, and they were very familiar with the idea of presenting sacrifices. The Law required them to make regular trips to the temple to present their sacrifices to the priests there. Paul used this picture of "presenting" throughout the book of Romans.

- In Romans 6:13, for what purpose does Paul want us to present ourselves to God?

- What imagery does Paul use in Romans 6:16 to describe the way we present our lives?

- According to Romans 6:19, we only have two choices in how our lives are lived. One way or the other, we are slaves. What are we slaves to?

> "So often we kick and scream at the thought of yielding. We don't want to give up control. If we could just understand that yielding to a benevolent and trustworthy 'other' can bring quietness, rest, and even happiness."
>
> Marilyn Meberg

3. What was Paul's goal in preaching the Gospel of Christ, according to Colossians 1:28?

> "When I find I am unable to yield a point or to yield to the spirit of Jesus, I ask myself: What am I holding on to? Why is it so difficult to simply yield, knowing full well that I will benefit from doing so?"
>
> Marilyn Meberg

4. What does Paul tell us to be diligent to do in 2 Timothy 2:15?

5. Jesus wants to present us to His Father one day.

- What did He do in order to make that possible, according to Colossians 1:22?

- How are we described during that presentation in Ephesians 5:27?

- In Jude 1:24, what exceeding emotion will the Lord (and we, too) be feeling in God's presence?

*T*here are times when it is really, really hard not to struggle. For instance, when I was a youngster taking swimming lessons, the instructor wanted to teach us how to rescue one another. The only way this worked was if the "rescue-ee" was willing to completely relax in the water, and allow the "rescue-er" to pull them along through the water to safety. "Stop thrashing about, and go limp," shouted the teacher, but it was so hard to give up the struggle and depend on someone else.

Another hard-fought struggle is that between a toddler and sleep. They'll rub their eyes, pull their ears, pinch themselves, and even start a fight with a friend just to keep moving. But in the end, they go limp—limp as a dishrag—and we can carry them off to get the rest they so desperately need. We, too, find ourselves struggling against the very thing we need most!

6. It's not easy to stop struggling. Even Jesus wrestled in prayer during His evening in the Garden of Gethsemane. "And being in agony, He prayed more earnestly. Then His sweat became like great drops of blood falling down to the ground" (Luke 22:44 NKJV). In spite of this, Jesus surrendered His will to His Father's. What does Luke 22:42 tell us Jesus said?

7. Surrender is the laying down of our lives. What did Jesus say He would do in John 10:15?

> *"Once I surrendered all to Jesus, I found His love to be lavish."*
>
> Thelma Wells

8. Of course, we don't always show Christ-like qualities. What was Peter's impassioned pledge in John 13:37? And what was Jesus' rejoinder in John 13:38?

9. What is the beloved disciple's admonition in 1 John 3:16?

DIGGING DEEPER

Jesus laid down His life for our sakes. He died in our place. But John tells us that we should be laying down our lives for each other. Not in death— this is a living sacrifice of sorts. What would you say is harder to do—to die for someone, or to live for them?

PONDER & PRAY

This week pray for a heart of surrender. Ask God to show you how to live with Him as Lord. Pray for the grace to "freely give" your all to God. Jesus died so that you could live. Tell Him now you want to live for Him.

TRINKETS TO TREASURE

Surrender is something our hearts seem to fight against. We long to give God our all, but to lay so much down at His feet—it can be very hard. Your trinket this week is a silly little reminder that you must stop fighting Him. It's a dishrag, and it's meant to nudge your memory with these few words: "Stop struggling! Go limp—limp as a dishrag!" Give your all to God and make our hymn your heartfelt song, "All to Jesus I surrender, all to Him I freely give."

NOTES & PRAYER REQUESTS

TAKING THE PLUNGE

"CHOOSE FOR YOURSELVES THIS DAY WHOM YOU WILL SERVE."

Joshua 24:15 NKJV

ave you ever learned to play chess? My father taught me when I was old enough to begin to grasp the strategy of the game. It wasn't an easy game to master. Every piece seemed to have a mind of its own, moving differently from the other pieces surrounding it. I dreaded losing pieces. I hated taking risks. I couldn't see the traps my father laid for me. I couldn't see past my next move, but he seemed to be omniscient as he commandeered his forces. With each move I grew more hesitant. I'd move my piece to a new square, but sit there for a minute or two, my fingertip stubbornly planted on top of it, trying to decide if I'd made a wise choice or if I'd put myself in danger. These games tended to be long, drawn out affairs which I rarely won.

My own skills with kings, queens, knights, bishops, rooks, and pawns stand in stark contrast with those of another man I once saw. He stood under a pavilion at a renaissance festival,

CLEARING ↗ THE ↖ COBWEBS

What kind of board games do you enjoy— word games, guessing games, strategy games, games of chance, games of logic?

surrounded by a square of tables set with some twenty chess sets. He was a slim, bearded bard of a man in leather breeches and a puffy-sleeved shirt. Challengers would take their place around the outside of the square, while he strode from board to board making his moves. It was one against twenty, and he was winning! With swift, confident assurance, he executed his strategy and dominated the matches.

I want to give God my all, to leap into His arms, to trust myself in His hands. I want to be confident, to throw all caution to the wind, to be changed. How I wish, in my Christian walk, I felt as confident as that chess master. But more often than not, I am the hesitant child with one finger holding me back from committing to anything.

1. You must decide. You must choose. What are you going to do—give God your all, or not? Choose Him, for He chose you! What does John 15:16 have to say on this subject?

2. He chose you! He wants you! Can you hold back your life from the One who saved it?

- What does Deuteronomy 14:2 call those who belong to God and are chosen by Him?

- According to Ephesians 1:4, when did God choose us as His own?

- What does Paul call us in 2 Thessalonians 2:13, and when does He say God chose us?

3. He chose you. He loves you. Can't you feel the tug at your heart? What does the Lord say to us in Jeremiah 31:3?

"My reluctance, my resistance, my disobedience frequently get in the way of my progress and growth."

Marilyn Meberg

4. We know that, "Blessed is the man You choose" (Ps. 65:4 NKJV). Are you still resisting? Have you manufactured some excuses? "I'm not important enough." "God doesn't need me." "I'm nobody!" But what does Paul tell us in 1 Corinthians 1:27–28?

> "What are you resisting? Has God been nudging you into action and you've either said 'no' repeatedly, or 'well, maybe' so weakly that no one can hear it? I can tell you from my own experience, the very thing we say 'no' to just might be God's blessing in disguise. He wants to bless us; He wants to mature us; He wants to get us out of our comfort zone."
>
> Luci Swindoll

5. What does 1 Peter 2:4 call those who are chosen by God?

6. What does 1 Peter 2:9 call us?

7. According to Revelation 17:14, what will those of us who are on the Lord's side be called?

*W*e use so many analogies to communicate this idea. Coming to a crossroads. Crossing the line. Turning a corner. Taking the plunge. Past the point of no return. Burning your bridges. No u-turns. We've even put this notion into song—one of the most famous songs of decision every written. "I have decided to follow Jesus. I have decided to follow Jesus. I have decided to follow Jesus; no turning back, no turning back." What is there left to say? There are only so many last minute instructions that can be given. You know what you need to know in order to do what you need to do. There's nothing left but the doing.

8. God chose us. We can choose Him. What did Joshua choose in Joshua 24:15?

> "Don't waste time holding yourself back from completely surrendering to God. God is love. He made you. He'll keep you. He won't give up on you. He has plans for you that will not harm you, but will give you a bright and glorious future."
>
> Thelma Wells

9. Another good example of choosing comes in Luke 10:42. What was chosen, and what promise was connected with that choice?

DIGGING DEEPER

We want to move forward with the Lord, giving Him our all without turning back. But before that can happen, often we must turn back to Him! "Turn us back to You, O Lord, and we will be restored" (Lam. 5:21 NKJV). Let's put it another way and make it our prayer: "Bring us back to you, God—we're ready to come back. Give us a fresh start" (MSG).

PONDER & PRAY

You are chosen by God! Pray this week for a heart and mind to comprehend the astonishing truth of this statement. Look back at what you've learned over the last several weeks, then take the plunge. After all, you know what you need to know in order to do what you need to do. Give God your all!

TRINKETS TO TREASURE

Have you chosen God? Have you decided to follow Him no matter what? Then your trinket this week will remind you of this. It's a "no u-turn" sign. As the hymn says, "I have decided to follow Jesus, no turning back." You can trust Him with all you have and all you are. You will never regret giving God your all.

NOTES & PRAYER REQUESTS

SHALL WE REVIEW?

1. A Shepherd's Crook

Sheep know and trust their shepherd, and we must learn to know and trust God completely before we can give Him our all. This trinket serves to remind us that God will always lead us aright.

2. A Feather Duster

When God's plans run contrary to our own, we need to submit to His will and let Him set the agenda. Rather than be impatient and impetuous, we need to rely on Him and trust the outcome to Him.

3. A Gold Coin

Our lives are no longer our own because we were bought with a great price. Jesus sacrificed His life for us. We can no longer live willfully for ourselves, but willing for the One who saved us.

4. A Loaf of Bread

We may not always feel that we have anything to offer the Lord, but when we give Him what we do have, He uses it for His glory. What can we give Him? Give Him our heart!

5. A Passport

Fear stands firmly in the way of our giving God our all. Few of us want to lose control of our lives, and are afraid of what God might ask of us. God might not send us all to far away places, but He may indeed ship us out of our comfort zones.

6. A Shield

This trinket was a simple reminder that God is faithful and we can trust Him. He is a shield to all who put their trust in Him.

7. A Bobber

Fishermen cast their lines. We are invited to cast our burdens, our cares, our fears, and our sorrows all on the Lord. This trinket was our reminder to place it all in God's hands.

8. A Packrat

Giving it all to God is one thing, leaving it there is another. Too often we're like packrats, hoarding our own problems and our own lives. Once we give something into the Lord's keeping, we mustn't try to scrounge it back up.

9. Baby Booties

When it seems like giving our all to God is just too difficult, and it's never going to happen, these booties can remind us that our spiritual walk begins with baby steps. When we hit a rough place, and want to cry out that it's too hard, we're experiencing growing pains, and must learn to trust God even more.

10. A Level

God's on the level. He's as good as His word. We can trust His character. We can depend on His promises. You cannot give yourself into the hands of one you do not trust, and you cannot trust one you do not know, so make it a point to get to know God through His Word.

11. A Dishrag

We need to surrender our lives to God, relinquishing our control and accepting His lordship. We struggle against such a choice, but this trinket reminds us, "Stop struggling! Go limp—limp as a dishrag!"

12. A "No U-Turn" Sign

Have you chosen God? Have you decided to follow Him no matter what? As the hymn says, "I have decided to follow Jesus, no turning back."

105

LEADER'S GUIDE

Chapter 1

1. "He who is the blessed and only Potentate, the King of kings and Lord of lords" (1 Tim. 6:15 NKJV). Potentate is just a fancy word for leader or ruler, like emperor or prime minister or president or king. Not only is God the "only Potentate," He is King over all earthly kings and Lord over all earthly lords. He tops them all. "For His is Lord of lords and King of kings" (Rev. 17:14 NKJV). "And He has on His robe and on His thigh a name written: KING OF KINGS AND LORD OF LORDS" (Rev. 19:16 NKJV). God has greater authority than the highest ruler in any land.

2. c, f, a, e, g, d, b

3. "Who may go out before them and go in before them, who may **lead** them out and **bring** them in, that the congregation of the Lord may not be like **sheep** which have no **shepherd**" (Num. 27:17 NKJV). "Give ear, O **Shepherd** of Israel, You who **lead** Joseph like a **flock**" (Ps. 80:1 NKJV). "He will **feed** His **flock** like a **shepherd**; He will **gather** the **lambs** with His arm, And **carry** them in His bosom, and **gently lead** those who are with young" (Is. 40:11 NKJV).

4. "Therefore the people wend their way like sheep; They are in trouble because there is no shepherd" (Zech. 10:2 NKJV). The picture here is of wandering, of just going with the flow of the other sheep.

5. "But when He saw the multitudes, He was moved with compassion for them, because they were weary and scattered, like sheep having no shepherd" (Matt. 9:36 NKJV). The people reminded the Lord of sheep, wandering around without anyone to guide them. They were scattered, lost, and oh so tired. Their weariness touched His heart.

6. "And when he brings out his own sheep, he goes before them; and the sheep follow him for they know his voice. Yet they will by no means follow a stranger, but will flee from him, for they do not know the voice of strangers" (John 10:4–5 NKJV). "My sheep hear My voice, and I know them, and they follow Me" (John 10:27 NKJV). Sheep may not know much, but there's one thing they do know. They know the voice of their own shepherd—the one they trust, and love, and follow. Jesus compares us with sheep, but offers to be our Shepherd. We can know His voice, trust His leading, and follow Him with confidence.

7. "I am the good shepherd. The good shepherd gives His life for the sheep . . . I am the good shepherd; and I know My sheep, and am known by My own" (John 10:11, 14 NKJV). Jesus is the Good Shepherd. "For you were like sheep going astray, but have now returned to the Shepherd and Overseer of your souls" (1 Pet. 2:25 NKJV). Again, we find the Lord called our Shepherd. He gathered us up when we were wandering, and He oversees the needs of our souls. "When the Chief Shepherd appears, you will receive the crown of glory that does not fade away" (1 Pet. 5:4 NKJV). Even in His coming, Peter calls Jesus the Chief Shepherd. Perhaps this is because, before Jesus returned to His Father in heaven, He charged Peter to "feed My lambs."

8. "I will bring the blind by a way they did not know, I will lead them in paths they have not known. I will make darkness light before them, And crooked places straight. These things I will do for them, And not forsake them" (Is. 42:16 NKJV). He will lead us when we cannot see our way. "They shall neither hunger nor thirst, Neither heat nor sun shall strike them; For He who has mercy on them will lead them, Even by the springs of water He will guide them" (Is. 49:10 NKJV). He leads us, and cares for our needs along the way. "The Lamb who is in the midst of the throne will shepherd them and lead them to living fountains of waters. And God will wipe away every tear from their eyes" (Rev. 7:17 NKJV). Even at the very end, Jesus will shepherd us, leading us into the glories of heaven.

9. "If anyone serves Me, let him follow Me; and where I am, there My servant will be also. If anyone serves Me, him My Father will honor" (John 12:26 NKJV). If you want to be where Jesus is, then follow Him there!

Chapter 2

1. "The wicked will go down to the grave. This is the fate of all the nations who ignore God" (Ps. 9:17 NLT). Just because folks ignore God doesn't mean He's not there. "Don't be misled. Remember that you can't ignore God and get away with it" (Gal. 6:7 NLT). I remember memorizing this verse in the KJV as a child: "Be not deceived, God is not mocked." Essentially, this verse says that we can't get away with anything because God knows our hearts and deeds, and there are consequences for disobedience. It reminds me of Jonah, who thought he could sneak out of town without God noticing. Who was he kidding?

2. "This is hopeless! So we will walk according to our own plans, and we will every one obey the dictates of his evil heart" (Jer. 18:12 NKJV). What honesty! Here are men who admit that they'd rather do their own thing. They have their own plans. They want to follow their own hearts.

3. I especially like how these three verses are rendered in the *New Living Translation*. "But all your feverish plans are to no avail because you never ask God for help. He is the one who planned this long ago" (Is. 22:11 NLT). How many of us forget even to include the Lord in our plans or ask for His help along the way? "Destruction is certain for those who try to hide their plans from the Lord, who try to keep him in the dark concerning what they do! 'The Lord can't see us,' you say to yourselves. 'He doesn't know what is going on!'" (Is. 29:15 NLT). It's useless to try to hide our plans from God. He knows our hearts, He sees our thoughts. We're deceiving ourselves if we think otherwise. "'Destruction is certain for my rebellious children,' says the Lord. 'You make plans that are contrary to my will. You weave a web of plans that are not from my Spirit, thus piling up your sins'" (Is. 30:1 NLT). God never pulls back from calling a spade a spade. We make plans according to our own agendas and ignore God's will in the process, and we're sinning. It's as simple as that.

4. "And now I say to you, keep away from these men and let them alone; for if this plan or this work is of men, it will come to nothing; but if it is of God, you cannot overthrow it—lest you even be found to fight against God" (Acts 5:38–39 NKJV). God's plans will prevail, whether we stand in their way or not. The Sadducees and Pharisees adopted a "wait and see" attitude towards these disciples of Jesus Christ. They assumed this new religion was a passing fad, borne of men, and would fizzle out.

5. "The Lord brings the counsel of the nations to nothing; He makes the plans of the peoples of no effect" (Ps. 33:10 NKJV). Everyone has plans for their life, but only those that line up with the Lord's will come to pass. The rest will fall aside, ineffectual. "A man's heart plans his way, But the Lord directs his steps" (Prov. 16:9 NKJV). Even as we plan the direction our lives will take, it is God who directs us along the way. He is the One who opens and closes doors and gives us the desires of our hearts. "There are many plans in a man's heart, Nevertheless the Lord's counsel—that will stand" (Prov. 19:21 NKJV). We usually have more plans than anyone could accomplish during a lifetime. God's way is as sure and true as He is.

6. "O Lord, my God, you have done many miracles for us. Your plans for us are too numerous to list. If I tried to recite all your wonderful deeds, I would never come to the end of them" (Ps. 40:5 NLT). David didn't seem to be put off by God's "meddling" in his life. He was pleased with all the things God had planned for him. In fact, he considered them "miraculous" and "wonderful!" David was thankful that God had numerous plans for him.

7. "The Lord will work out his plans for my life—for your faithful love, O Lord, endures forever. Don't abandon me, for you made me" (Ps. 138:8 NLT). God is working out His plans in our lives. Why? Because of His great love for us!

8. "The counsel of the Lord stands forever, The plans of His heart to all generations" (Ps. 33:11 NKJV). God's plan will be completed—it will stand. Nothing can shove it off course. And His plan is big! It spans all the generations of mankind that ever have and ever will be.

9. "'For I know the plans I have for you,' says the Lord. 'They are plans for good and not for disaster, to give you a future and a hope'" (Jer. 29:11 NLT). God's plans are for our good. Better yet, this verse has such a personal note—"I know you. I have a plan for you." And He makes us a thrilling promise. We will have a future and a hope.

Chapter 3

1. "That he no longer should live the rest of his time in the flesh for the lusts of men, but for the will of God" (1 Pet. 4:2 NKJV). Peter is straightforward enough. What should we live for? We should live to do the will of God.

2. "I have found David the son of Jesse, a man after My own heart, who will do all My will" (Acts 13:22 NKJV). We always hear the phrase, "a man after God's own heart," used. But seldom do we see its accompanying phrase—"who will do all My will." Why was David so close to God's heart? Because he was willing to do God's will!

3. Jesus said, "Not My will, but Yours, be done" (Luke 22:42 NKJV). The Perfect Man had the perfect attitude. Even when He was faced with the prospect of pain and suffering and humiliation and death, He was willing to put God's plans over His own desires.

4. "For whoever does the will of God is My brother and My sister and mother" (Mark 3:35 NKJV). Jesus tells us that if we do the will of God, we're family! We're His sisters and His mothers! "The world is passing away, and the lust of it; but he who does the will of God abides forever" (1 John 2:17 NKJV). What a promise! Those who do the will of God will abide forever.

5. "Not with eyeservice, as men-pleasers, but as bondservants of Christ, doing the will of God from the heart" (Eph. 6:6 NKJV). We don't live our lives to please the people who might see us and praise us for our good moral behavior. We live before God, and it's His opinion that matters! The willful heart follows its own wishes and whims, but the willing heart seeks to do the will of God *wholeheartedly*!

6. "Do you thus deal with the Lord, O foolish and unwise people? Is He not your Father, who bought you? Has He not made you and established you?" (Deut. 32:6 NKJV). God bought His people—redeemed them. "You were bought at a price; do not become slaves of men" (1 Cor. 7:23 NKJV). What's the word? Bought. Our lives were bought at a price, and a high price indeed! Jesus' life was traded for our own, and His pain and suffering and shed blood were the cost of our freedom. "You were bought at a price; therefore glorify God in your body and in your spirit, which are God's" (1 Cor. 6:20 NKJV). Because we belong to God, we're able to bring glory to His name through our lives.

7. "Christ has redeemed us from the curse of the law, having become a curse for us" (Gal. 3:13 NKJV). The price of our salvation? Jesus' life, His blood.

8. "I have **blotted out**, like a thick **cloud**, your **transgressions**, And like a **cloud**, your **sins**. Return to Me, for I have **redeemed** you" (Is. 44:22 NKJV). "But now, thus says the Lord, who **created** you, O Jacob, And He who **formed** you, O Israel: 'Fear not, for I have **redeemed** you; I have **called** you by your **name**; You are **Mine**'" (Is. 43:1 NKJV). "My **lips** shall **greatly rejoice** when I **sing** to You, And my **soul**, which You have **redeemed**" (Ps. 71:23 NKJV).

9. "As for you, my son Solomon, know the God of your father, and serve Him with a loyal heart and with a willing mind; for the Lord searches all hearts and understands all the intent of the thoughts. If you seek Him, He will be found by you; but if you forsake Him, He will cast you off forever" (1 Chr. 28:9 NKJV). Look at this checklist! Know God. Serve Him. Have a loyal heart. Have a willing mind. Seek God!

Chapter 4

1. "Well then," he said, "give to Caesar what belongs to him. But everything that belongs to God must be given to God" (Matt. 22:21 NLT). We must give to God what belongs to Him!

2. "We give glory to God through Christ" (2 Cor. 1:20 NLT). We give God glory. In fact, that is the very purpose of our lives—to glorify God. "You will always give thanks for everything to God the Father in the name of our Lord Jesus Christ" (Eph. 5:20 NLT). We owe God our thanks, and should never take His blessings for granted.

3. "And now, Israel, what does the Lord your God require of you, but to fear the Lord your God, to walk in all His ways and to love Him, to served the Lord your God with all your heart and with all your soul, and to keep the commandments of the Lord and His statutes which I command you today for your good?" (Deut. 10:12–13 NKJV). What does God want? Seems He wants it all! Respect, obedience, love, willing service. And He wants us to give these things willingly from our hearts—with all our heart and all our soul. Other verses include all our mind and all our strength. So if we go back to the original question, of just what belongs to God, we could say that *we* do, part and parcel!

4. "Then they will not be like their ancestors—stubborn, rebellious, and unfaithful, refusing to give their hearts to God" (Ps. 78:8 NLT). Not a very flattering description, is it? David looks back at a people who would not put themselves into God's hands. They wouldn't trust Him, wouldn't obey Him, wouldn't give Him their allegiance. And so their legacy is one of censure—stubborn, rebellious, unfaithful.

5. "You will **seek** the Lord your God, and you will **find** Him if you **seek** Him with all your heart and with all your soul" (Deut. 4:29 NKJV). "You shall **love** the Lord your God with all your heart" (Deut. 6:5 NKJV). "To **serve** the Lord your God with all your heart and with all your soul" (Deut. 10:12 NKJV). "**Return** to the Lord your God and **obey** His voice . . . with all your heart and with all your soul" (Deut. 30:2 NKJV). "**Turn** to the Lord your God with all your heart and with all your soul" (Deut. 30:10 NKJV). "With all my heart I will **praise you**" (Ps. 86:12 NLT). "**Search** for Me with all your heart" (Jer. 29:13 NKJV).

6. "Remember that you must give an account to God for everything you do" (Eccl. 11:9 NLT). "But I say to you that for every idle word men may speak, they will give account of it in the day of judgment" (Matt. 12:36 NKJV). "Yes, each of us will have to give a personal account to God" (Rom. 14:12 NLT). Yes, we are forgiven. Yes, we are redeemed. Yes, by grace we are saved by faith. But Scripture also says that we will be held accountable for how we lived our lives. Someday, we will have to give an account to the Lord.

7. "Do not let any part of your body become a tool of wickedness, to be used for sinning. Instead, give yourselves completely to God since you have been given new life. And use your whole body as a tool to do what is right for the glory of God" (Rom. 6:13 NLT). Give yourselves completely to God!

8. "And so, dear brothers and sisters, I plead with you to give your bodies to God. Let them be a living and holy sacrifice—the kind he will accept. When you think of what he has done for you, is this too much to ask?" (Rom. 12:1 NLT). Paul compares the giving of our lives to God to a sacrifice—living, holy, and acceptable. Sacrifices involve some cost to ourselves. That reminds me of a line from a song, "I will not offer anything that cost me nothing."

9. "Then I will give them a heart to know Me, that I am the Lord; and they shall be My people, and I will be their God, for they shall return to Me with their whole heart" (Jer. 24:7 NKJV). "I will give you a new heart and put a new spirit within you; I will take the heart of stone out of your flesh and give you a heart of flesh" (Ezek. 36:26 NKJV). "Take delight in the Lord, and he will give you your heart's desires" (Ps. 37:4 NLT). Giving our all to God isn't such an easy thing to do, but if we ask Him, God can change our hearts. He makes us willing.

Chapter 5

1. "All things were made through Him, and without Him nothing was made that was made" (John 1:3 NKJV). There is nothing in all of creation that was not made by God. "He gives to all life, breath, and all things" (Acts 17:25 NKJV). We would not have life or breath if it were not for the Lord. "For of Him and through Him and to Him are all things, to whom be glory forever. Amen" (Rom. 11:36 NKJV).What a poetic way to put it! "From Him, through Him, to Him." "For by Him all things were created . . . All things were created through Him and for Him" (Col. 1:16 NKJV). We were not only created by God, but we were created *for* God.

2. "With men this is impossible, but with God all things are possible" (Matt. 19:26 NKJV). There is nothing God cannot do, so long as it is in line with His character.

3. d, g, a, f, b, h, e, c

4. "He who did not spare His own Son, but delivered Him up for us all, how shall He not with Him also freely give us all things?" (Rom. 8:32 NKJV). What a startling bit of logic. God, who didn't withhold His Son's own life for our sakes, will surely not withhold from us anything we might need. Will the God who did not withhold His only Son draw the line at some small request we might make? Paul assures us that God is ready and willing to give us what we need. "I can do all things through Christ who strengthens me" (Phil. 4:13 NKJV). "His divine power has given to us all things that pertain to life and godliness" (2 Pet. 1:3 NKJV). God, in His great power, has given us everything we shall need for our lives and for godliness.

5. "We know that all things work together for good to those who love God, to those who are the called according to His purpose" (Rom. 8:28 NKJV). Here are some of the most famous and hope-filled words of the New Testament. In times of great pain, they may seem like empty platitudes, but this is the very promise we can and must cling to when we cannot understand what's going on. This is the promise that someday we will look back and understand. This is the promise that through it all, God is good and good will come.

6. "In Him also we have obtained an inheritance, being predestined according to the purpose of Him who works all things according to the counsel of His will, that we who first trusted in Christ should be to the praise of His glory" (Eph. 1:11–12 NKJV). There are some very key phrases in this sentence. Things happen according to God's purposes. What's more, God is described as "Him who works all things according to the counsel of His will." Not only does God have a plan, He's in the process of working it out!

7. "If anyone speaks, let him speak as the oracles of God. If anyone ministers, let him do it as with the ability which God supplies, that in all things

God may be glorified through Jesus Christ" (1 Pet. 4:11 NKJV). No matter what happens in our lives, our words and deeds should glorify God.

8. "But as for you, you meant evil against me; but God meant it for good" (Gen. 50:20 NKJV). We say hindsight is twenty-twenty. Joseph was able to look back without malice at what his brothers had done because He saw God's hand in the circumstances. "Indeed it was for my own peace that I had great bitterness" (Is. 38:17 NKJV). Or as another translation puts it, "Yes, it was good for me to suffer this anguish" (NLT). We don't like to hear that something rather unpleasant is "for our own good," but there you have it. "I want you to know, brethren, that the things which happened to me have actually turned out for the furtherance of the gospel" (Phil. 1:12 NKJV). Paul's life was filled with apparent mishaps and upsets and drama and pain. But Paul was convinced that even these "regrettable" circumstances turned out to be the very best thing that could have happened to him, because they spread the gospel message.

9. No one likes the thought of going through the fire, even if the end result is a promise of coming forth like gold. We want the results of God's finishing work in our lives, but we'd like to do it without any inconvenience or discomfort on our part. Many of the men and women in Scripture had to do scary things. Some lost their lives. Some lost those closest to them. Some endured injustice, shame, scrutiny, criticism, and the dreaded unknown for God's sake. We are secretly afraid God might ask something similar of us.

Chapter 6

1. "You believe in God, believe also in Me" (John 14:1 NKJV). Jesus asks His followers to believe in Him. He asks them to trust Him, to take His word for it. "These are written that you may believe that Jesus is the Christ, the Son of God, and that believing you may have life in His name" (John 20:31 NKJV). God's Word helps our belief, and that belief brings us life—eternal life! "When you received the word of God which you heard from us, you welcomed it not as the word of men, but as it is in truth, the word of God, which also effectively works in you who believe" (1 Thess.

2:13 NKJV). Paul says that God's Word works in our hearts. God uses it to change our hearts and our lives.

2. "Those who know Your name will put their trust in You; For You, Lord have not forsaken those who seek You" (Ps. 9:10 NKJV). We know God, true enough. But we also must put our trust in Him.

3. "But as for me, I trust in You, O Lord; I say, 'You are my God'" (Ps. 31:14 NKJV). David is bold and clear in his statement. You are my God. I trust You.

4. **Psalm 62:8** — Trust God all the time. Tell Him what's in your heart, because He's your safe place. **Psalm 20:7** — Don't put your trust in earthly things. Trust in God alone. **Psalm 36:7** — We trust God because of His lovingkindness toward us. **Psalm 52:8** — We can trust in God's mercy forever. **Psalm 64:10** — Those who trust in the Lord will be glad in Him. **Psalm 71:5** — I have trusted God since I was a child, and my hope is in Him. **Psalm 73:28** — I will draw near to the God I trust. **Proverbs 3:5** — I trust God more than I trust my own understanding. I'll lean on Him. **Isaiah 12:2** — Because I trust God, I do not need to be afraid.

5. e, a, g, b, h, c, f, d

6. "He knows those who trust in Him" (Nah. 1:7 NKJV). God knows our hearts. He knows exactly who trusts Him.

7. "Oh taste and see that the Lord is good" (Ps. 34:8 NKJV). This verse almost seems like a challenge for us to find out for ourselves just how far we can trust God. "Taste and see." Try it and see! Give Him a chance to prove Himself faithful!

8. "Commit your way to the Lord, Trust also in Him, And He shall bring it to pass" (Ps. 37:5 NKJV). Trust God. Commit your way to Him. Choose to follow Him. Give yourself wholeheartedly to Him. Make His plans your plans. Follow Him.

Chapter 7

1. "The haters of the Lord would pretend submission to Him" (Ps. 81:15 NKJV). These people pretend to follow God—pretend to live their lives for Him even while they do just as they please. "Therefore submit to God" (James 4:7 NKJV). Our lives are meant to be lived in submission to God. He is, after all, our Lord. "Father, if it is Your will, take this cup away from Me; nevertheless not My will, but Yours, be done" (Luke 22:42 NKJV). Jesus modeled this perfect submission to God in His life and death. Even when faced with life-and-death choices, Jesus submitted His will to God's.

2. "Casting all your care upon Him, for He cares for you" (1 Pet. 5:7 NKJV). One way of looking at things is that we're giving up our will in order to do God's, and that seems like a great sacrifice. But if you look at it another way, when we give our lives to God, He also takes on our troubles for us. God takes care of those who are His. He invites us to cast our cares upon Him!

3. "Oh, what a sinful nation they are! They are loaded down with a burden of guilt. They are evil and corrupt children who have turned away from the Lord. They have despised the Holy One of Israel, cutting themselves off from his help" (Is. 1:4 NLT). What colorful, descriptive words! Loaded down, burdened, evil, corrupt, and turning away. These are the characteristics of those who are sinning.

4. g, d, a, b, f, i, e, h, c

5. "Now I will relieve your shoulder of its burden; I will free your hands from their heavy tasks" (Ps. 81:6 NLT). God takes on our burdens. He frees us from heavy tasks.

6. "For My yoke is easy and My burden is light" (Matt. 11:30 NKJV). Will we live as slaves to sin or slaves to God? Jesus tells us that while following Him means taking on a different sort of servitude, the yoke we must bear is an easy one.

7. "You saw how the Lord your God carried you, as a man carries his son, in all the way that you went until you came to this place" (Deut. 1:31 NKJV). God cares for us as a man does for his son. "He will feed His flock like a shepherd; He will gather the lambs with His arm, And carry them in His bosom, And gently lead those who are with young" (Is. 40:11 NKJV). God carries, feeds, and gently leads those who belong to Him. "Even to your old age, I am He, And even to gray hairs I will carry you! I have made, and I will bear; Even I will carry, and will deliver you" (Is. 46:4 NKJV). Even into our old age, God carries us along. His care of us lasts our whole life long!

8. "Surely He has borne our griefs And carried our sorrows; Yet we esteemed Him stricken, Smitten by God, and afflicted" (Is. 53:4 NKJV). Not only does God carry our burdens and cares for us. Here we find that He is able to carry our griefs and sorrows. In those times when our need is greatest, God is our greatest comfort.

9. "Save Your people, And bless Your inheritance; Shepherd them also, And bear them up forever" (Ps. 28:9 NKJV). Save us. Bless us. Shepherd us. Bear us up forever.

Chapter 8

1. "As far as the east is from the west, So far has He removed our transgressions from us" (Ps. 103:12 NKJV). When we say God takes our sins away, this verse gives us some idea of just how far away! "You have cast all my sins behind Your back" (Is. 38:17 NKJV). He casts them away. "I will forgive their iniquity, and their sin I will remember no more" (Jer. 31:34 NKJV). God promises that when He forgives our sins, they are both forgiven and forgotten.

2. My people are bent on backsliding from Me. Though they call to the Most High, None at all exalt Him" (Hos. 11:7 NKJV). We sometimes hear of people who have backslidden in their faith. Many of us may not realize this is a Scriptural term!

3. b, e, a, f, d, c

4. "The Lord swore to David a promise he will never take back" (Ps. 132:11 NLT). God never goes back on His word. When He says He will do something, He does it. We may often say we want to give God our all, but just as often we struggle with the frustration of failing to follow through. We go back on our word. We slide back into old habits.

5. "No one, having put his hand to the plow, and looking back, is fit for the kingdom of God" (Luke 9:62 NKJV). This verse reminds me of Paul's words—"I do not count myself to have apprehended; but one thing I do, forgetting those things which are behind and reaching forward to those things which are ahead" (Phil. 3:13 NKJV). We, too, must press on!

6. "As a dog returns to his own vomit, So a fool repeats his folly" (Prov. 26:11 NKJV). Ewwwwww! God help us, we all stumble at times. But if we do not learn from our mistakes, we're called fools. Thank the Lord for the forgiveness, patience, grace, and mercy that are ours in this life! The moment we turn to Him for help and forgiveness, He is there!

7. "But it has happened to them according to the true proverb: 'A dog returns to his own vomit,' and 'a sow, having washed, to her wallowing in the mire'" (2 Pet. 2:22 NKJV). Alright, the dog thing was bad enough. But none of us wants to be compared with a pig wallowing in mud. However, there's a good reason why this is called a "true proverb." We know ourselves too well to deny it. It happens to us all. Good intentions, New Year's resolutions, best-laid plans—they so easily end in nothing. The same is true for our desire to put our lives wholly into God's hands. It's too easy to snatch our lives back! It's too easy to backslide! So we are always consciously putting our lives back where they belong. One day at a time, one hour at a time, one moment at a time we commit ourselves to God.

8. "The way of life winds upward for the wise, That he may turn away from hell below" (Prov. 15:24 NKJV). Instead of going one step forward and two steps back, with the Lord's help we'll make two steps forward for every one step back. The path will never be easy, but our progress will be steady if, with the Lord's own help, we persevere.

9. "Turn away my eyes from looking at worthless things, And revive me in Your way" (Ps. 119:37 NKJV). We put our lives in God's hands, and we must learn to leave them there. God is able to revive us when we find we cannot do this in our own strength. The God who never turns back from His promises helps us not to turn back or slide back on the upward way!

Chapter 9

1. "For I know that in me (that is, in my flesh) nothing good dwells; for to will is present with me, but how to perform what is good I do not find" (Rom. 7:18 NKJV). Or put more simply in *The Message's* paraphrase: "I realize that I don't have what it takes. I can will it, but I can't do it."

2. "See that no one renders evil for evil to anyone, but always pursue what is good both for yourselves and for all" (1 Thess. 5:15 NKJV). Pursue what is good!

3. e, a, h, f, c, d, g, b (I know, I know—*e* and *b* are interchangeable. That's because Peter quotes the psalm!)

4. The passages quoted from *The Message* appeared in this order: Romans 15:3, Philippians 3:18–19, Acts 14:22, 1 Thessalonians 5:3, 1 Corinthians 7:35.

5. "He who endures to the end shall be saved" (Matt. 24:13 NKJV). If we endure we will be saved. That's where the whole, "it'll be worth it" comes in! "If anyone's work which he has built on it endures, he will receive a reward" (1 Cor. 3:14 NKJV). We all build on the foundation God has laid in our lives. Some of us build shaky structures, and others of us have learned what will endure. This verse uses this picture to tell us that those who have chosen to build their lives around things that endure will be rewarded. "You therefore must endure hardship as a good soldier of Jesus Christ" (2 Tim. 2:3 NKJV). Paul calls up military imagery in his illustration here. "If we endure, We shall also reign with Him. If we deny Him, He also will deny us" (2 Tim. 2:12 NKJV). What an amazing promise. Those who endure will reign with Christ! "Indeed we count them blessed who endure" (James 5:11 NKJV). We who endure are counted as blessed.

6. "Yet he has no root in himself, but endures only for a while. For when tribulation or persecution arises because of the word, immediately he stumbles" (Matt. 13:21 NKJV). Other translations say, "Their roots don't go very deep. At first they get along fine, but they wilt as soon as they have problems or are persecuted because they believe the word" (NLT). "He does not let the teaching go deep into his life, so he keeps it only a short time. When trouble or persecution comes because of the teaching he accepted, he quickly gives up" (NCV). "But there is no soil of character, and so when the emotions wear off and some difficulty arrives, there is nothing to show for it" (MSG).

7. "That Christ may dwell in your hearts through faith; that you, being rooted and grounded in love" (Eph. 3:17 NKJV). Our foundation, our source of strength, the ground into which we anchor and root ourselves is God and His great love for us.

8. "Do not boast against the branches. But if you do boast, remember that you do not support the root, but the root supports you" (Rom. 11:18 NKJV). When we're struggling with our Christian walk, and long to give up because it's just too hard, it helps to remember that we really cannot do it all in our own strength. Just as the branches cannot boast because they could do nothing without the root, we cannot do anything without the Lord. God is our source of strength.

9. "The root of the righteous cannot be moved" (Prov. 12:3 NKJV). When we depend upon God, we cannot be shaken by our circumstances. "The root of the righteous yields fruit" (Prov. 12:12 NKJV). We will not wither away as soon as struggles come our way. We are supported by our roots, flourish, and bear fruit to God's glory.

Chapter 10

1. No matter what colloquialism we may use to say it, the truth of the matter remains steady. God never lies. God always does what He says. God always tells the truth. God is always faithful. We can trust such a One to take care of us if we put our lives in His hands.

2. Deuteronomy 4:31 — God is merciful. Psalm 68:20 — God is the God of salvation. John 3:33 — God is true. John 4:24 — God is spirit. 1 Corinthians 1:9 — God is faithful. 1 John 1:5 — God is light. 1 John 4:16 — God is love.

3. "The Lord your God is a consuming fire, a jealous God" (Deut. 4:24 NKJV). God wants us to love Him wholeheartedly. He will not share our affections with another, lesser idol. "God is our refuge and strength, A very present help in trouble" (Ps. 46:1 NKJV). God is our safe place and source of strength in hard times. "For God is the King of all the earth" (Ps. 47:7 NKJV). Men may set themselves up as monarchs or dictators, but in the end, God's sovereignty is universal! "For the Lord God is a sun and shield" (Ps. 84:11 NKJV). God is the brightness of light, and whether in battle or in defense, His shield cannot be breeched.

4. "For the Lord your God is **God** of **gods** and **Lord** of **lords**, the **great** God, **mighty** and **awesome**, who shows no **partiality**" (Deut. 10:17 NKJV). "Be **strong** and of good **courage**; do not be **afraid**, nor be **dismayed**, for the Lord your God is **with** you **wherever** you go" (Josh. 1:9 NKJV). "Behold, God is **exalted** by His **power**; Who **teaches** like Him?" (Job 36:22 NKJV).

5. f, a, h, i, b, k, d, c, j, e, g

6. 2 Samuel 22:33 — God is my strength and power. Psalm 54:4 — God is my helper. Psalm 73:26 — God is my portion forever. Psalm 59:17 — God is my defense, my God of mercy. Psalm 62:7 — God is my salvation and my glory, the rock of my strength, and my refuge. Psalm 74:12 — God is my King from of old.

7. "Behold, God is great, and we do not know Him; Nor can the number of His years be discovered" (Job 36:26 NKJV). The simple fact is that God is beyond our understanding. We cannot fully understand Him. Even those things He *has* revealed about Himself boggle our minds!

8. "The foolishness of God is wiser than men, and the weakness of God is stronger than men" (1 Cor. 1:25 NKJV). God is far and away more wise, good, and sure than we will ever be. If we had to put all our eggs into one basket, so to speak, we should put them in His! God is as good as His word, and His promises to us are plentiful and precious. Him we can know. Him we can trust.

9. "The hand of our God is upon all those for good who seek Him" (Ezra 8:22 NKJV). We cannot deny that God has His hand in our lives. Though we may resist Him, He is still sovereign. But we can always, always be confident that God's hand is upon us for good. We can trust God, we can trust His plans, we can trust His motives. We can know with certainty that all things work together for good.

Chapter 11

1. "I **beseech** you therefore, **brethren**, by the **mercies** of God, that you **present** your **bodies** a **living sacrifice**, **holy**, **acceptable** to God, which is your **reasonable service**" (Rom. 12:1 NKJV).

2. "Do not present your members as instruments of unrighteousness to sin, but present yourselves to God as being alive from the dead, and your members as instruments of righteousness to God" (Rom. 6:13 NKJV). "Do you not know that to whom you present yourselves slaves to obey, you are that one's slaves whom you obey, whether of sin leading to death, or of obedience leading to righteousness?" (Rom. 6:16 NKJV). There's really no middle ground! We may balk at the idea of becoming a slave or sacrifice to God, but if we resist Him, we're only making ourselves slaves to sin. "For just as you presented your members as slaves of uncleanness, and of lawlessness leading to more lawlessness, so now present your members as slaves of righteousness for holiness" (Rom. 6:19 NKJV). Don't balk at surrendering yourselves to God and presenting your life to Him. We're slaves no matter how we look at it, but we can choose the master we want to serve. Besides, the Lord elevates His servants to sons and daughters!

3. "Him we preach, warning every man and teaching every man in all wisdom, that we may present every man perfect in Christ Jesus" (Col. 1:28 NKJV). Paul preaches and teaches and warns all who will listen to him with one goal in mind—being able to present men and women to God once they've been made righteous through salvation. When we know Jesus, we are justified—made perfect in God's eyes. Only then can we come to God and find welcome.

4. "Be diligent to present yourself approved to God, a worker who does not need to be ashamed, rightly dividing the word of truth" (2 Tim. 2:15 NKJV). Present yourselves approved to God. Live before God in a way that is pleasing to Him. And what's more, be diligent in doing so. Diligence is needed!

5. "In the body of His flesh through death, to present you holy, and blameless, and above reproach in His sight" (Col. 1:22 NKJV). Jesus' death made our presentation to God a reality. "That He might present her to Himself a glorious church, not having spot or wrinkle or any such thing, but that she should be holy and without blemish" (Eph. 5:27 NKJV). We are called glorious, and described as clean, bright, and perfect. In other passages, this is accompanied with a comparison to a bride. "Now to Him who is able to keep you from stumbling, and to present you faultless before the presence of His glory with exceeding joy" (Jude 1:24 NKJV). Jesus will present us with joy—exceeding joy!

6. "Father, if it is Your will, take this cup away from Me; nevertheless not My will, but Yours, be done" (Luke 22:42 NKJV). Other translations reword this famous declaration slightly. "Do what you want, not what I want" (NCV). "But please, not what I want. What do you want?" (MSG). The idea of surrender, relinquishment, submission, willingness are beautifully portrayed in Christ as He faces the Cross.

7. "As the Father knows Me, even so I know the Father; and I lay down My life for the sheep" (John 10:15 NKJV). The willingness to sacrifice Himself for the sake of His flock was the distinguishing characteristic of the Good Shepherd. Jesus was willing to surrender His life so that we could have eternal life.

8. "Peter said to Him, 'Lord, why can I not follow You now? I will lay down my life for Your sake.' Jesus answered him, 'Will you lay down your life for My sake? Most assuredly, I say to you, the rooster shall not crow till you have denied Me three times'" (John 13:37–38 NKJV). Aren't we often just like Peter? Filled with enthusiasm we make undying pledges to God. "I'll read more, I'll pray more, I'll serve more, I'll love more! I give my life to You!" And yet before we've even turned around, everything we intended to surrender is snatched back up into our own hands. But the Lord understands. He forgave Peter. He forgives us. And He's still able to use our lives for His glory.

9. "By this we know love, because He laid down His life for us. And we also ought to lay down our lives for the brethren" (1 John 3:16 NKJV). Jesus lived and died all so that we could be saved. Now that we have been saved, we are asked to return the favor by living for Him.

Chapter 12

1. "You did not choose Me, but I chose you and appointed you that you should go and bear fruit, and that your fruit should remain, that whatever you ask the Father in My name He may give you" (John 15:16 NKJV). We are chosen. In fact, we were chosen by Jesus before we ever chose Him! Not only that, we were chosen for a purpose—to bear good and lasting fruit.

2. "For you are a holy people to the Lord your God, and the Lord has chosen you to be a people for Himself, a special treasure" (Deut. 14:2 NKJV). Those who belong to God are His own special treasure. Originally, this only included the Jews, but we Gentiles can be grateful that we've been "grafted in." "He chose us in Him before the foundation of the world, that we should be holy and without blame before Him in love" (Eph. 1:4 NKJV). Though it boggles the mind to consider it, God knew us and chose us before the foundations of the world were laid. "We are bound to give thanks to God always for you, brethren beloved by the Lord, because God from the beginning chose you for salvation through sanctification by the Spirit and belief in the truth" (2 Thess. 2:13 NKJV). Paul calls us "beloved by the Lord," and says that from the very beginning we've been chosen.

3. "The Lord has appeared of old to me, saying: 'Yes I have loved you with an everlasting love; Therefore with lovingkindness I have drawn you'" (Jer. 31:3 NKJV). The Lord is drawing us to Himself. He knows our fears and our reluctance to give Him our all, but He coaxes us to trust Him by love and kindness.

4. "God has chosen the foolish things of the world to put to shame the wise, and God has chosen the weak things of the world to put to shame the things which are mighty; and the base things of the world and the things which are despised God has chosen, and the things which are not, to bring to nothing the things that are" (1 Cor. 1:27–28 NKJV). We've no real excuses. None of us is too weak, too simple, or too humble for God to use us. In fact, the more unworthy we feel, the more qualified we are!

5. "Chosen by God and precious" (1 Pet. 2:4 NKJV). In this case, Peter is speaking of Jesus, but the same could be applied to each of us. If we are chosen by God, we are precious to Him. "Red and yellow, black and white, we are precious in His sight!"

6. "You are a chosen generation, a royal priesthood, a holy nation, His own special people" (1 Pet. 2:9 NKJV). Chosen, royal, holy, special. I especially like the *King James Version's* reference to us as "peculiar people."

7. "These will make war with the Lamb, and the Lamb will overcome them, for He is Lord of lords and King of kings; and those who are with Him are called, chosen, and faithful" (Rev. 17:14 NKJV). We are referred to as the called, the chosen, and the faithful.

8. "Choose for yourselves this day whom you will serve . . . But as for me and my house, we will serve the Lord" (Josh. 24:15 NKJV). Joshua stands up before the people and basically says, "You have a choice to make. Will you serve God or not? You all can choose whatever you want to do, but as for me, I choose God!" We, too, can take a stand and choose to give our all to God.

9. "One thing is needed, and Mary has chosen that good part, which will not be taken away from her" (Luke 10:42 NKJV). Most of the things we run across in our days will not last beyond this life on earth. Creature comforts are optional. The only things that are needed are the things that cannot be taken away from us. Mary seems to have sensed this. Martha did not, for life's practical necessities had overwhelmed her. Martha wanted to give the Lord a hot meal and a cold drink. Mary wanted to give the Lord all her time and attention. She was willing to give her all. And that changed everything.

Printed in the USA
CPSIA information can be obtained
at www.ICGtesting.com
JSHW030747140724
66378JS00008B/92

9 780310 682639